LAST HOUSE STANDING

How Once We Looked: Photographs of the Past

michael philip manheim
PHOTOGRAPHY

SEE-SAW

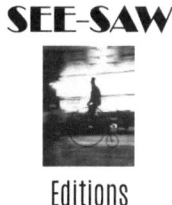

Editions

BY MICHAEL PHILIP MANHEIM

IN A LABYRINTH
LAST HOUSE STANDING, A Chapter
SEE-SAW, A Sampler
THE SMOKING FIFTIES
WHERE MY SPIRIT GUIDES US

These can be found on Amazon by entering Michael Philip Manheim in the search field

LAST HOUSE STANDING
A chapter — in the 1970s Segment — of
How Once We Looked

For further information or permissions, including the leasing of reproduction rights, go to
www.michaelphilipmanheim.com and click on "contact me"

Printed in the United States of America.

ISBN-13: 978-0-9844803-5-7

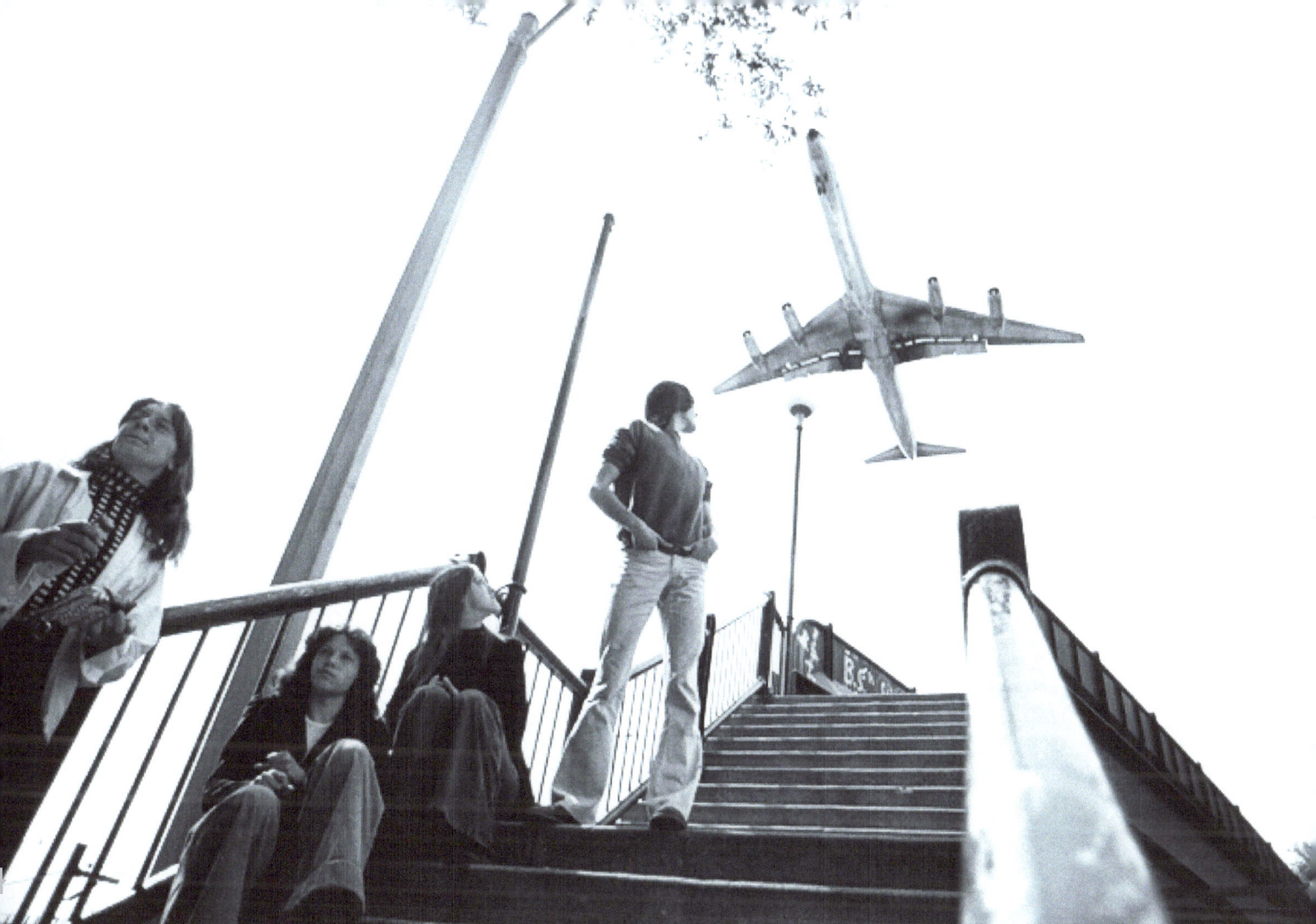

Last House Standing

Sandra Bruno (seated, facing camera) and friends pause in conversation as high decibels drown out any attempts at communication. They have gathered at a pedestrian bridge that went over the rapid transit tracks, as the Blue Line subway emerged from a tunnel to cut across Neptune Road. The other end of Neptune was cut off by the airport. These teens seem to accept the high noise levels although it can be speculated that their hearing might be impaired. Most significant: their world had been bordered by uncaring development. And then obliterated.

Last House Standing

East Boston, Massachusetts was once bucolic, a place where people would find relief from a stifling summer downtown. Wood Island Park was one of its magnets, located off Neptune Road, with acres of trees and grass, ending at the Atlantic and its ocean breezes. Wood Island Park was designed by Frederick Law Olmsted and treasured as one of his green spaces.

"Vast salt marshes once covered most of East Boston and the Dorchester shoreline, meadows dotted the hilltops of Roxbury, and pristine streams coursed through the forests of Hyde Park and West Roxbury. Although almost all significant portions of these habitats have been lost due to extensive human-induced manipulation of land and water, remnants of these original ecosystems—urban wilds—still dot the landscape and provide brief glimpses of the natural world."[1]

That is the enlightened view of today. In 1904 progress was represented by a subway tunnel connecting East Boston to the rest of the city. An airfield built in the early 1920s expanded into what is today's Logan International Airport. It became the 20th busiest airport in the U.S., even while lacking the land mass of other major airports. Logan is almost completely surrounded by water, which limits its growth.

Rather than utilize it as a feeder airport, officials expanded into East Boston, wiping out Wood Island Park and impacting the community with aircraft flights low overhead that at times resembled bombing raids. Construction sent noisy trucks through the streets. Taxis and busses and shuttle vans serviced the airport and added to the din.

In 1948 Boston's first expressway was conceived, to connect the airport with downtown Boston. This highway cut through East Boston, dividing the community by cutting off the Neptune Road neighborhood and creating an elevated eyesore. When the subway expanded above ground, it cut off one end of Neptune Road as a further insult to neighborhood integrity.

---

1. Official site of the City of Boston, "Urban Wilds," https://www.cityofboston.gov/parks/urbanwilds (accessed 20 June 2014).

Eventually, this encroaching civilization destroyed a close-knit, well-cared-for neighborhood community. When I photographed residents trying to hang on, in the early 1970s, it was already too late. The powers that be had made decisions that literally kept hammering away at the neighborhood. As an example, there was the morning that residents of Neptune Road awakened to even more construction noise. This time the other end of their street, now pointing directly at a runway, was fenced off. Logan Airport expanded right into the neighborhood. Power dominated private and pleasant life.

On revisiting Neptune Road in 2010 and again in 2013, I found little evidence of the life that had once flourished here: street signs, some lampposts, a fire hydrant, trees, and not much more. It was a poignant scene.

And yet those photographs from 1973 might have some purpose today. They appeared too late to save Neptune Road. But they still carry a message. The philosopher George Santayana once observed, "Those who cannot remember the past are condemned to repeat it."

Perhaps, in these more awakened times, any civic group threatened by an overreaching metropolis might think to access the DOCUMERICA files of my images.[2] These photographs could bolster a case of how tragic it would be if their own local treasures were abolished. Perhaps the power of photography might serve to dramatize the worthiness of quality of life.

---

2. Michael Philip Manheim, "See-Saw Explained," http://www.michaelphilipmanheim.com/see-saw/news.php (accessed 20 June 2014).

DOCUMERICA Revisited

I was commissioned, in 1973, by the newly minted Environmental Protection Agency (along with close to 70 other photographers) to document the multitude of environmental issues facing our nation. Gifford Hampshire and Arthur Rothstein recruited me for my phase of the project.

I had been following newspaper reports about the environmental impact of the Logan Airport expansion on East Boston. I knew that taking on this project would be challenging. A major part of the East Boston dilemma was noise pollution, which is difficult to capture in still photographs. But the subject called me. It underscored how the dominant wield their power, to the detriment of quality of life.

There was much publicity at the time. Then the DOCUMERICA photographs went into the National Archives, tucked away in archival storage for forty years until it was recovered and resurrected through a team of public servants. Jeanethe Falvey, then of the EPA, led the way bringing the project and its purpose back, sparking renewed public awareness.

In the course of this, Jeanethe reached out for my piece of the puzzle, and put its modern iteration, "State of the Environment Photography Project," into motion.[3] Here was a visual reminder that we must persevere in saving the earth. Those of us touched by DOCUMERICA hope that it serves as a reminder of what once was, and what may yet be done. It is a reminder that our choices make a difference.

2011 marked the 40th anniversary of DOCUMERICA. Due in no small part to Falvey's efforts, the National Archives rekindled the project, presenting a retrospective exhibit to highlight the photography started by the EPA's Gifford Hampshire.

Hampshire's idea was to put qualified photographers out into the field, to document facets of what was there. He told us to "remember that all these environmental problems had a human side to them . . . that we were trying to show the human condition that the environmental conditions were causing."

My photography was included in an anniversary exhibit at the National Archives in Washington D.C., and I took part in a panel discussion there. Linda Wertheimer moderated with her usual keen insights and observations, and our conversation got pretty lively . . . and poignant. It gave me new urgency to publish my collection and share one neighborhood's story of loss and collapse in the hopes of sparking new interest in how to prevent such calamities in the future.

As I review the images and captions I created, my heart again goes out to the good people I documented (now scattered) who were just wanting to go on with their lives.

— Michael Philip Manheim

---

3. Flickr, "State of the Environment Photography Project," https://www.flickr.com/groups/ourenvironment (accessed 20 June 2014).

Editor's Note:

For the DOCUMERICA Project (1971-1977), the Environmental Protection Agency (EPA) hired freelance photographers to capture images relating to environmental problems, EPA activities, and everyday life in the 1970s.

Michael Philip Manheim was one of approximately seventy well-known photographers hired for DOCUMERICA. His assignment was to document the noise pollution crisis in the East Boston neighborhood around Neptune Road.

Manheim captured powerful images of the deteriorating community, illustrating its uncomfortable proximity to one of the nation's busiest airports and the plight of residents living directly under the flight paths of airplanes on Logan's 15/33 runway. He ended up covering not only that, but all the other intrusions afflicting the Neptune Road area.

When the pictures were posted to Flickr forty years later, Manheim saw a real and vital interest in the work, prompting him to author this book.

Impact of Logan on the Neptune Road Neighborhood, East Boston, Massachusetts

John Vitagliano, in his paper "Logan Then & Now 1959-1985," gives an excellent review of the events leading up to the pollution and eventual demise of the Neptune Road Neighborhood and its inhabitants.

INTRODUCTION

Thanks to an abundance of promotional efforts from many sources, including Massport, it is fairly common knowledge that Logan International Airport is one of Massachusetts' most important economic assets. Logan handles more than 20 million passengers and close to 600 million pounds of cargo annually, generating thousands of jobs while providing New England with an essential link to the rest of the nation and the world.

While the benefits and advantages of Logan are well-documented and widely recognized, there has been an unfortunate shortage of published information about the severe cultural, social and economic costs that have accompanied development at Logan -- costs that have been absorbed by many densely populated residential communities and that continue to accrue to this day. Because Logan's development and operational costs have never been offset by adequate compensatory programs, it is fair to say that Logan Airport has been -- and continues to be -- subsidized by the unpaid debts owed to its neighboring communities.

It is my hope that this document will lend a degree of balance to other Logan publications that ignored the events contained here, and that it provides some enlightenment to those who question the depth of emotion that characterizes the protests of Logan's neighbors.

John Vitagliano

John Vitagliano
Vice Chairman of the Board
Massport

"Those who cannot remember the past are condemned to repeat it."

- G. Santayana

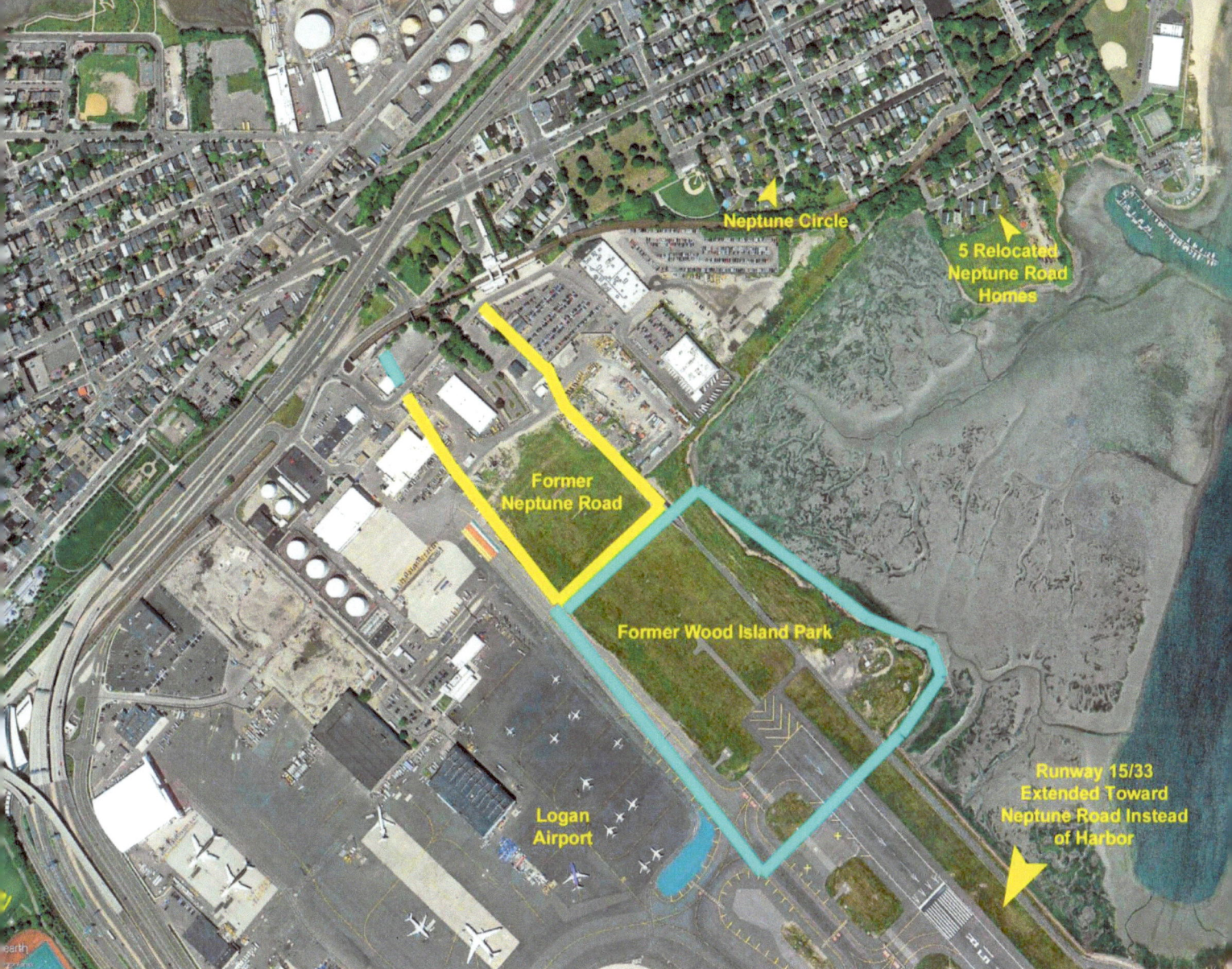

When John Vitagliano was on the Massport board, a great effort was made to help residents. The board even moved five of the three-decker homes and built new homes for other neighborhood residents. But diaspora never replaced the close-knit former neighborhood.

1 a neighborhood

2 the sound of progress

3 last house standing

1 a neighborhood

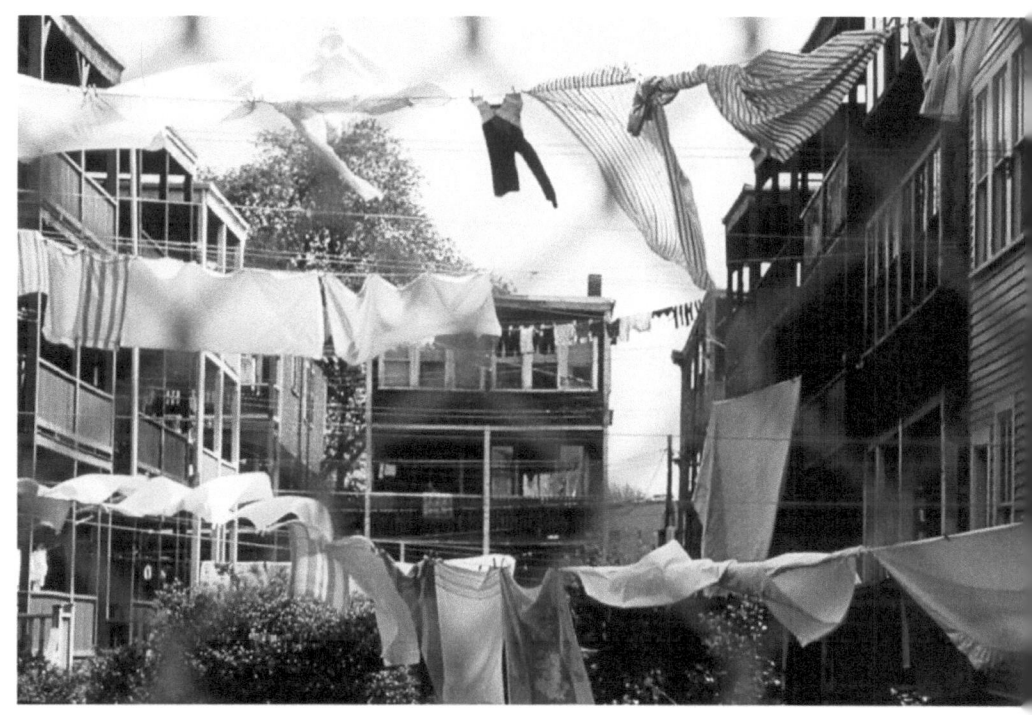

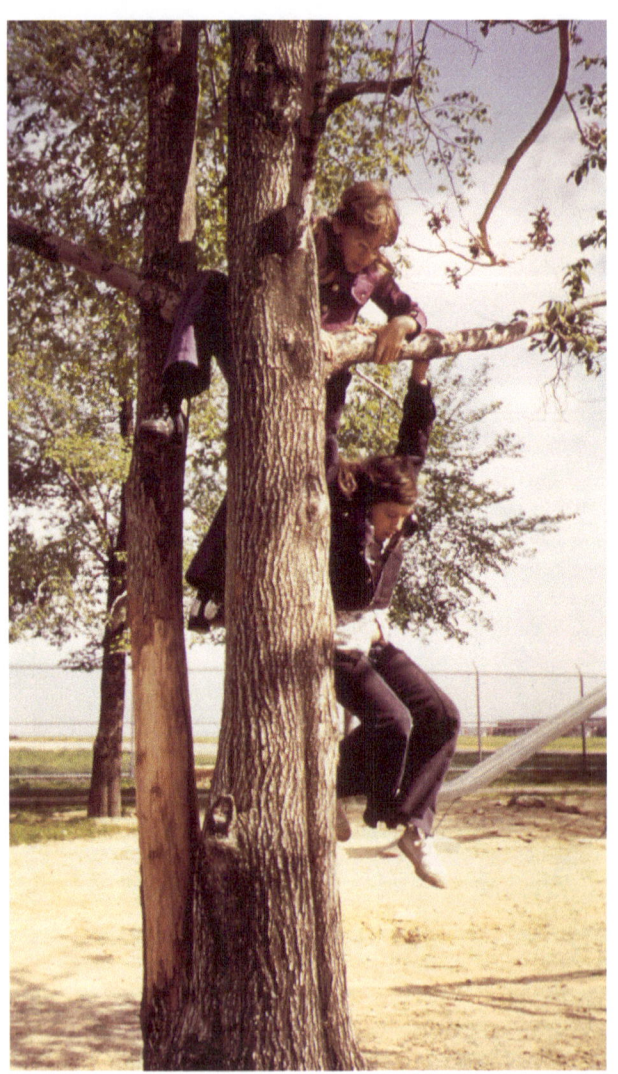

What price quality of life, anywhere in
the world, when those in power act
solely on their own desires.
They attempt to dominate, with actions
that obliterate the peaceful living of
others.

— Michael Philip Manheim

At the time, the Neptune Road neighborhood was a densely populated residential enclave on 5.5 acres of land surrounded by Logan Airport on three sides. 178 families lived in 66 privately-owned houses, representing a total of between 400 to 500 adults and children. Located less than 2,000 feet from the actual threshold of Logan's runway 15R, and directly under the flight path, noise levels in the Neptune Road area were extremely high. The severe noise impact, as well as the potential safety hazard of living in what would normally be declared a "clear zone", were the principal reasons Massport initiated the Neptune Road Relocation Program. On August 16, 1973, the Massport Board voted to undertake the purchase of homes and the relocation of residents with the Federal Relocation Act as a guideline.

— John Vitagliano, "Logan Then & Now 1959-1985"

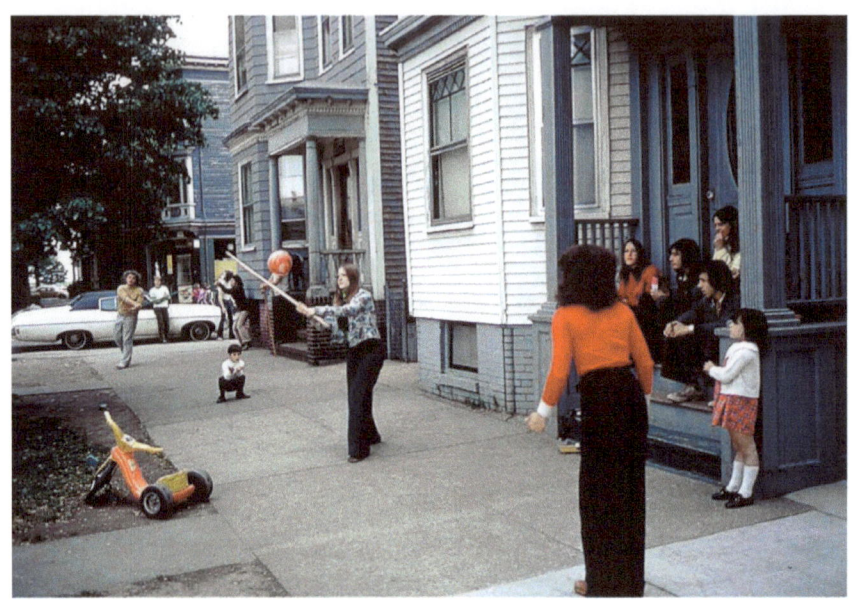

They had a village, a neighborhood of East Boston three-deckers where everybody knew everybody, kids played safely, and adults mentored and kept an eye on them.

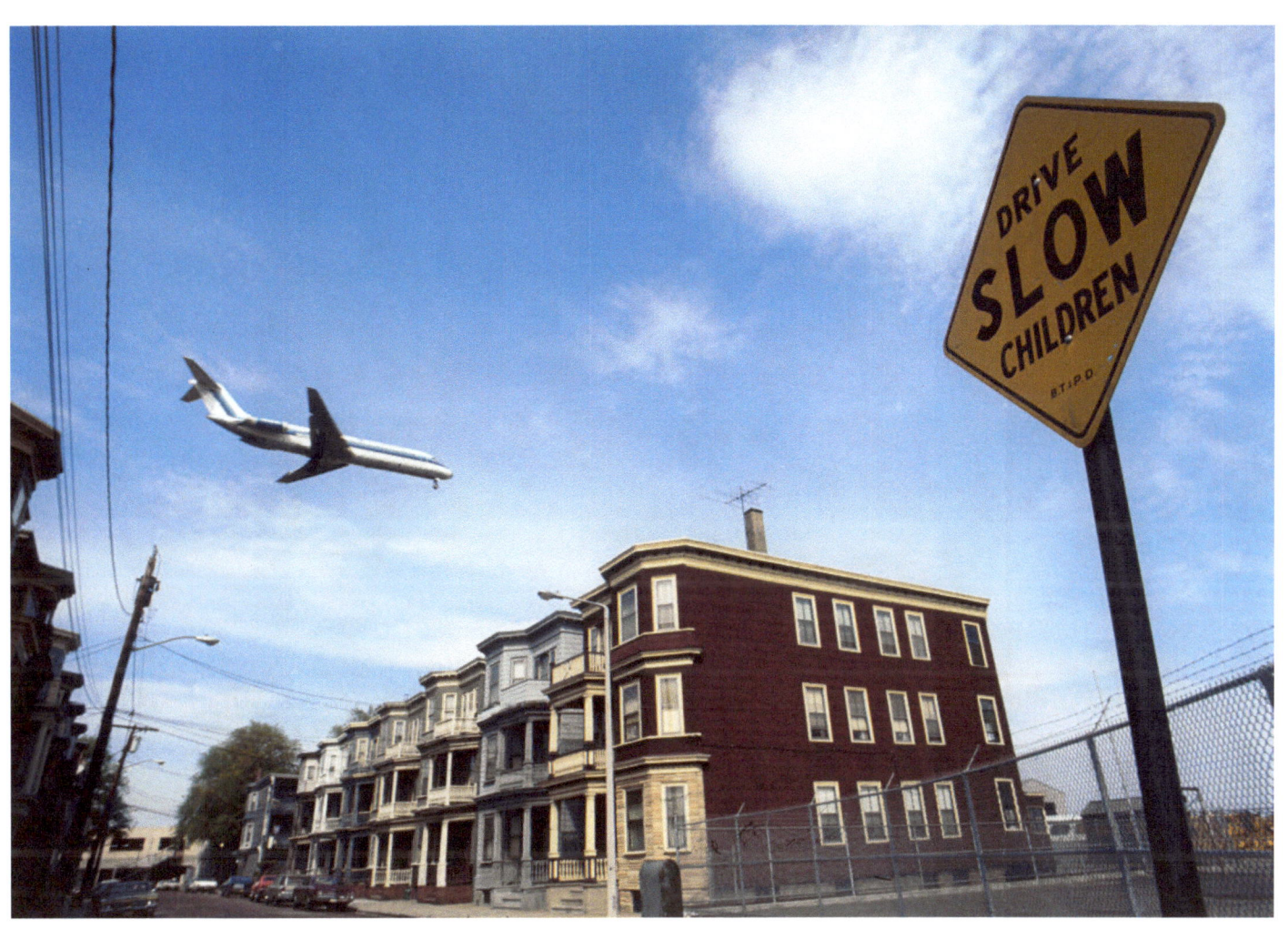

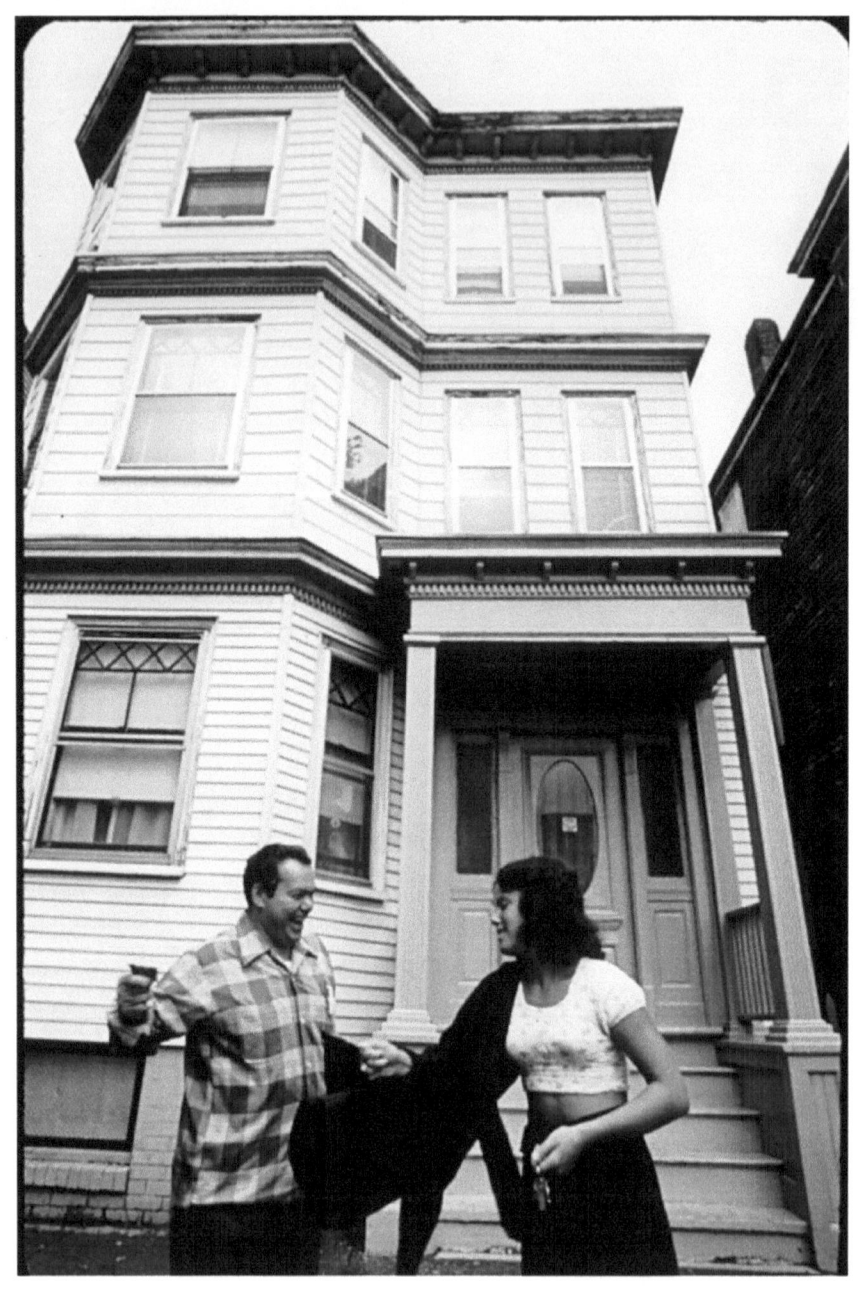

Father and daughter in front of a typical three-decker:
Anthony Bruno and daughter Sandra at their 39 Neptune Road home.

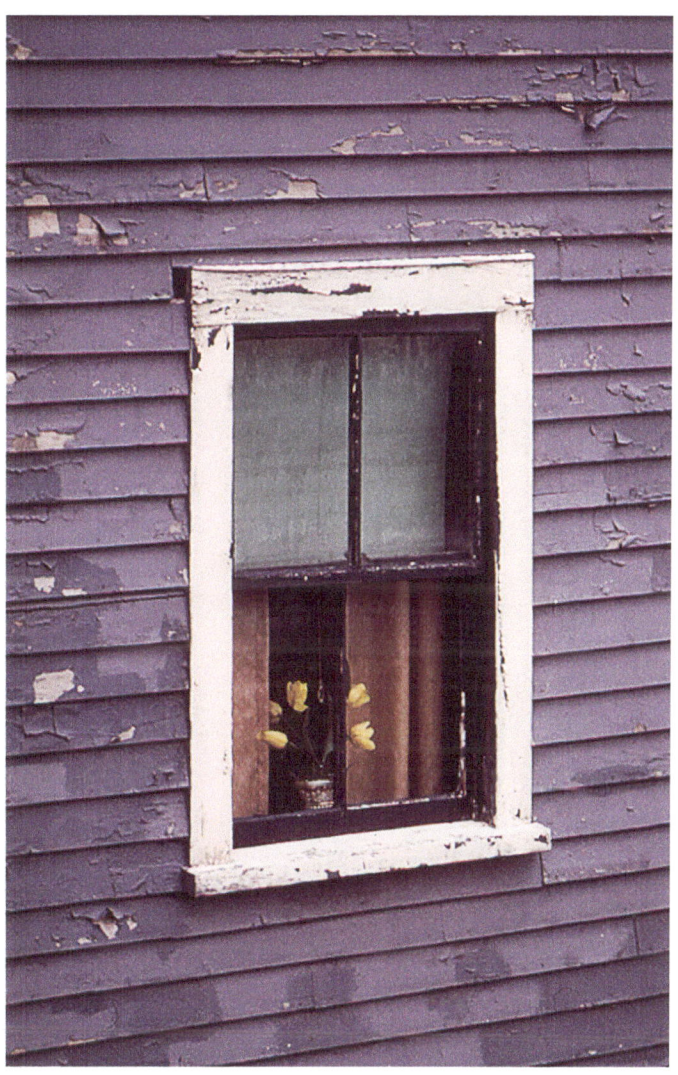

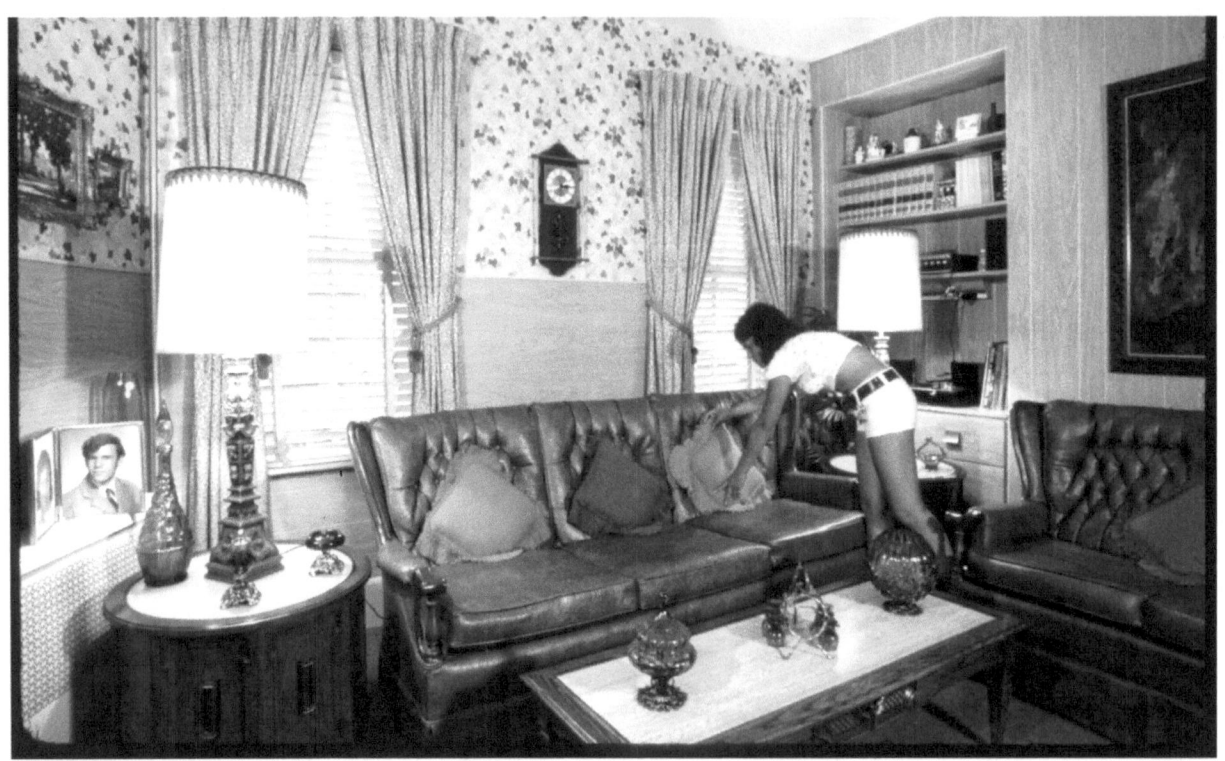

Under threat of airport expansion, residents gave up maintaining the exteriors of their structures. But inside was immaculate, well-cared-for living. Here, Sandra Bruno straightens up the family living room. As was typical in three-deckers, owners would take one floor and rent out the other two. The homes were once proud showplaces along a street which ran to the sea. The street extended into Wood Island Park and its 70 acres of recreational area which terminated at the Atlantic Ocean.

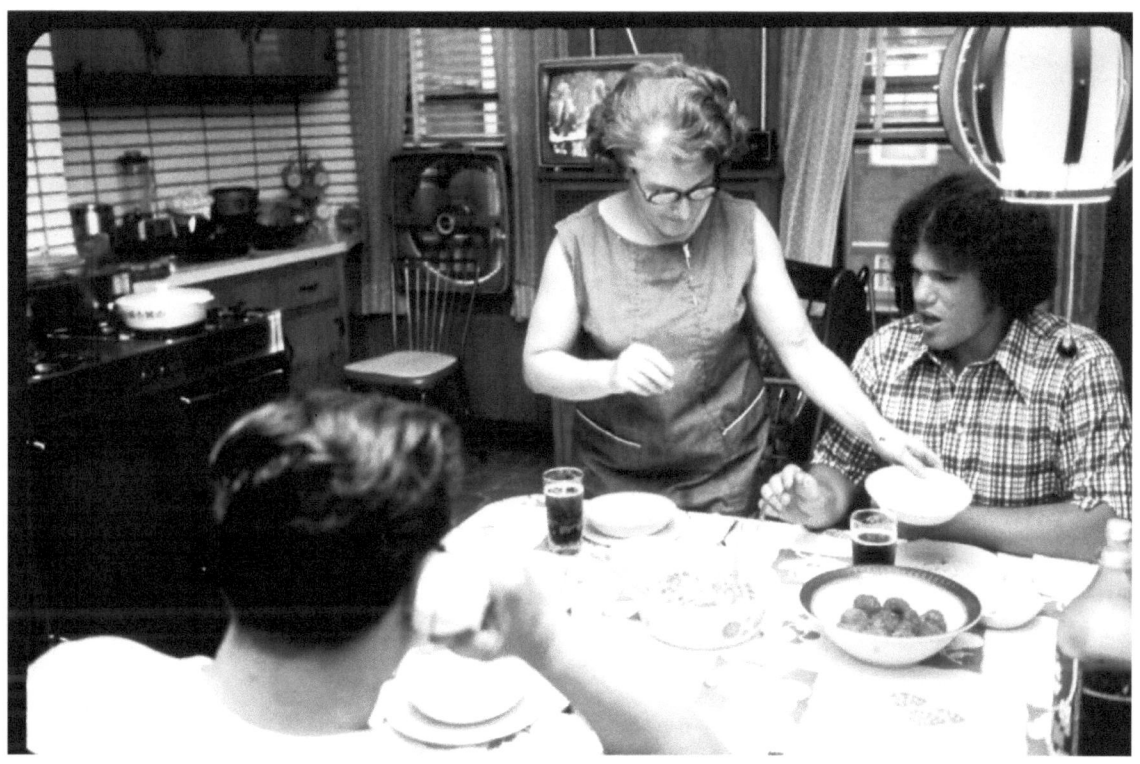

Mary Bruno serves dinner to husband Anthony, who was a high school teacher of law, and son Anthony L., Jr. who was working in the foreign currency department of the then First National Bank, in Boston.

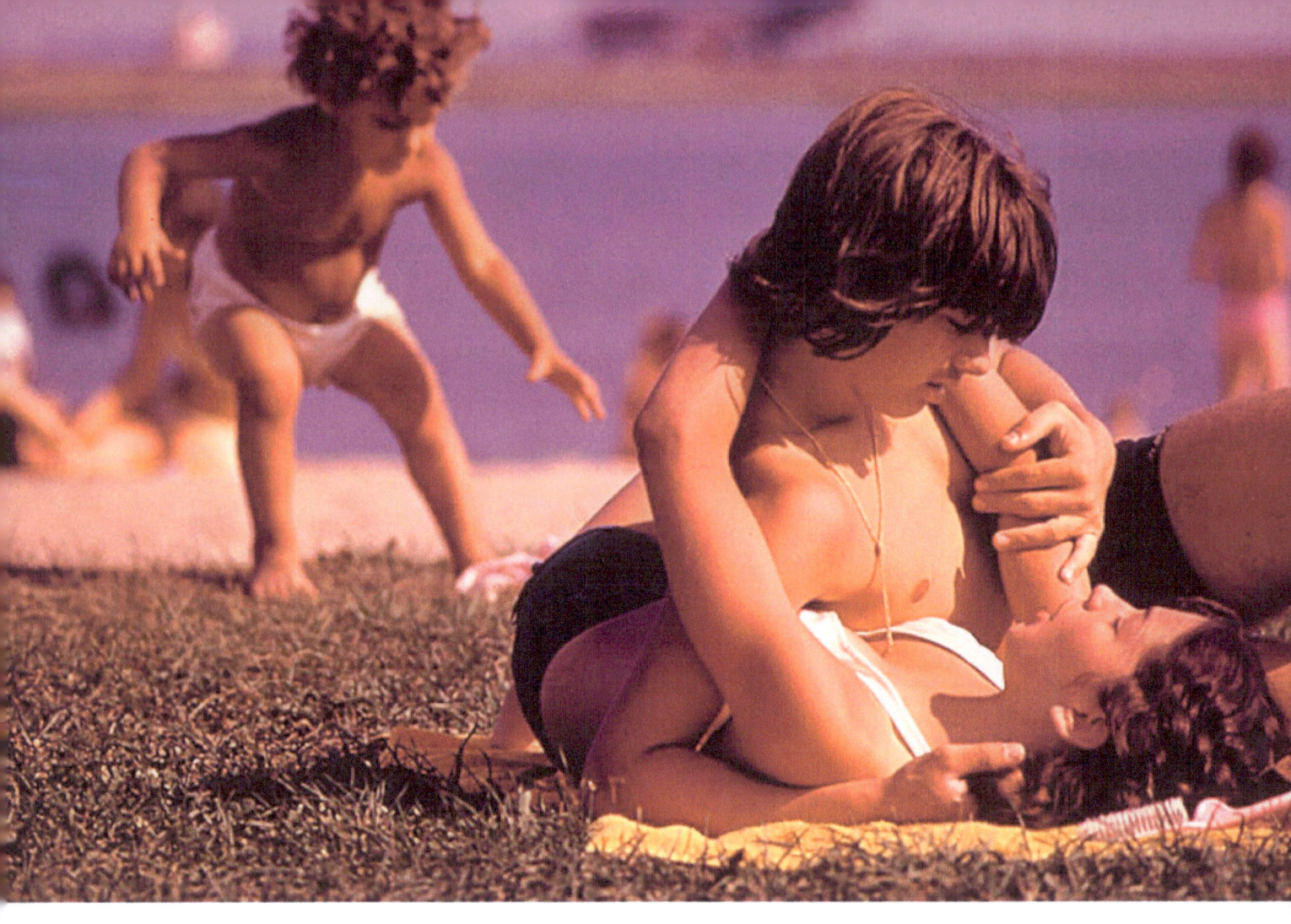

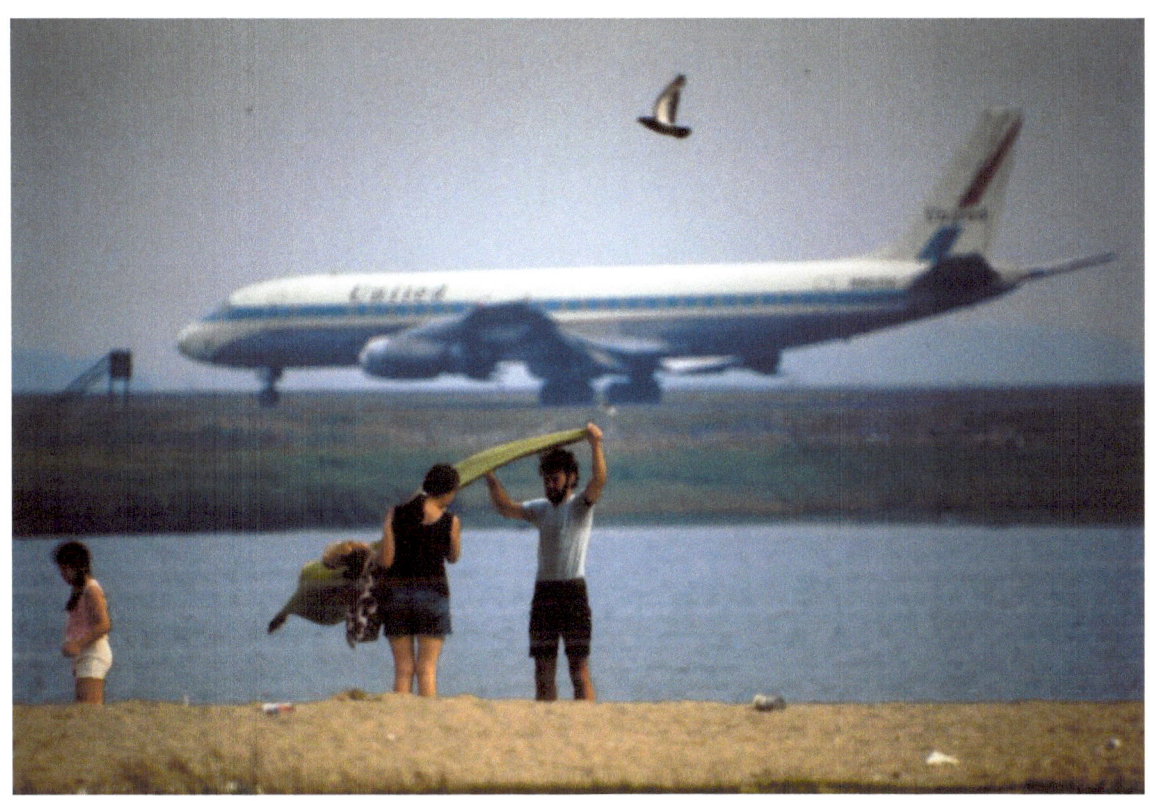

As the airport expanded, with resultant noise and air pollution, residents tried their best to maintain normalcy, including here at Constitution Beach, within walking distance from Neptune Road. The area at the ocean's edge was Wood Island Park, one of the Olmstead designs where in earlier times residents from the heart of Boston would escape the summer heat.

2 the sound of progress

THE NEPTUNE ROAD PROPERTY
ACQUISITION AND RELOCATION PROGRAM

In September of 1972, a group of Neptune Road residents
petitioned Massport for relief from aircraft noise levels and
the potential hazards represented by aircraft passing less than
100 feet over their homes. The petition was presented shortly
after the Massport Board had voted to discontinue all
off-airport property purchases because of community criticism.
These residents alleged that their neighborhood was a special
situation--and it was.

— John Vitagliano, "Logan Then & Now 1959-1985"

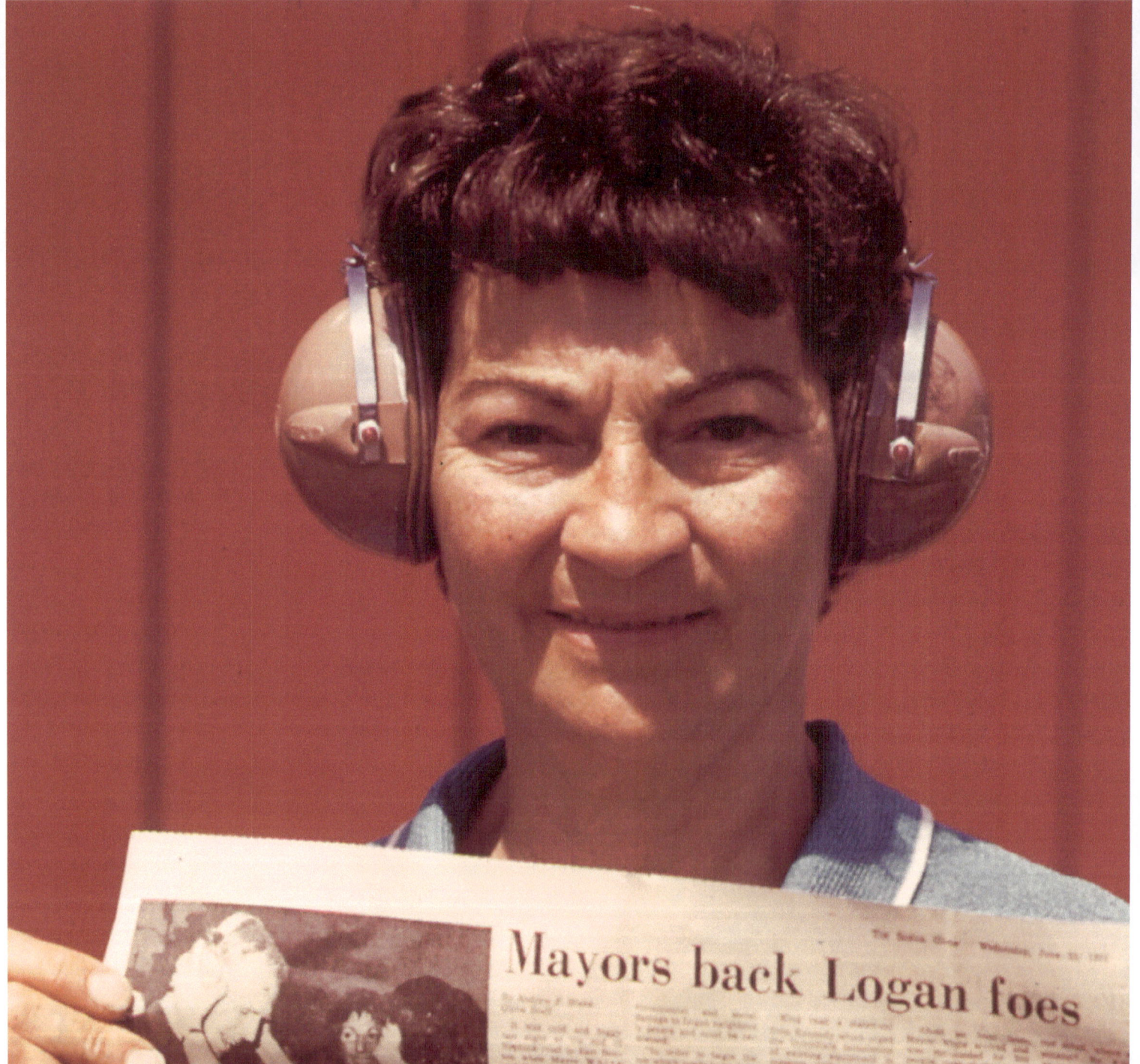

Mayors back Logan foes

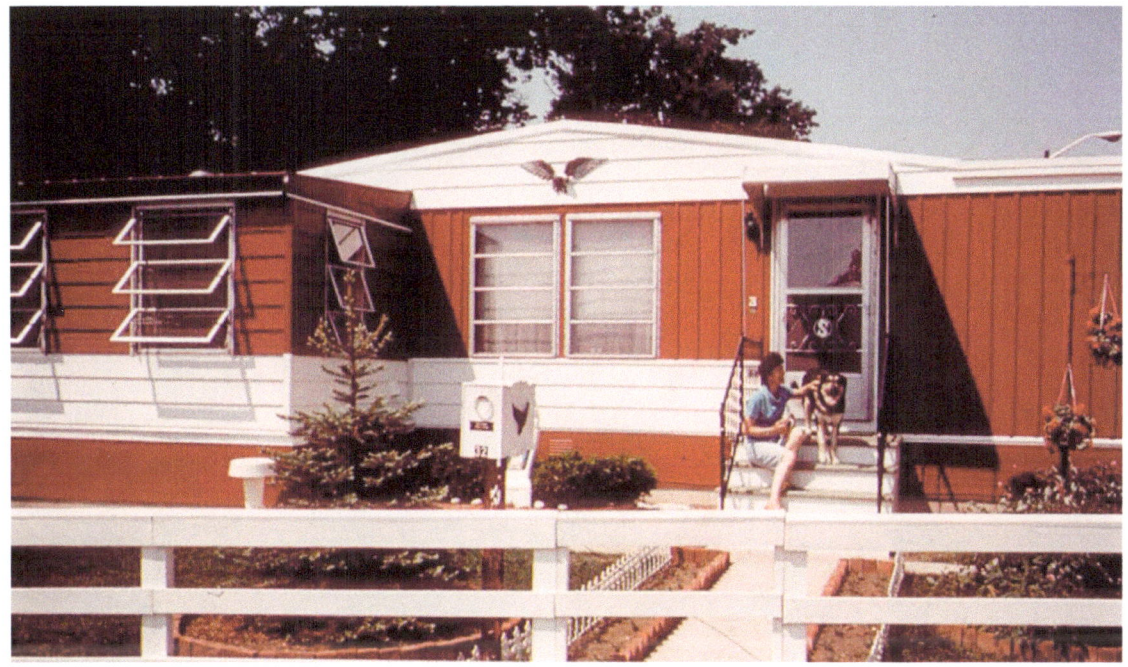

Massport authorities systematically bought out homeowners such as Mary Stack, who tired of having to wear the doctor-recommended noise-suppressing headset shown here. She moved with her husband to this scaled-down home in a mobile park in Saugus MA, some ten miles north of East Boston.

An East Boston newspaper claimed that Massport was generous in having just bought a three-decker for $30,000 because its original purchase price was $5,000. The problems: 1) value was severely depreciated because of the pollution problems. 2) it didn't approximate current prices in finding a comparable structure.

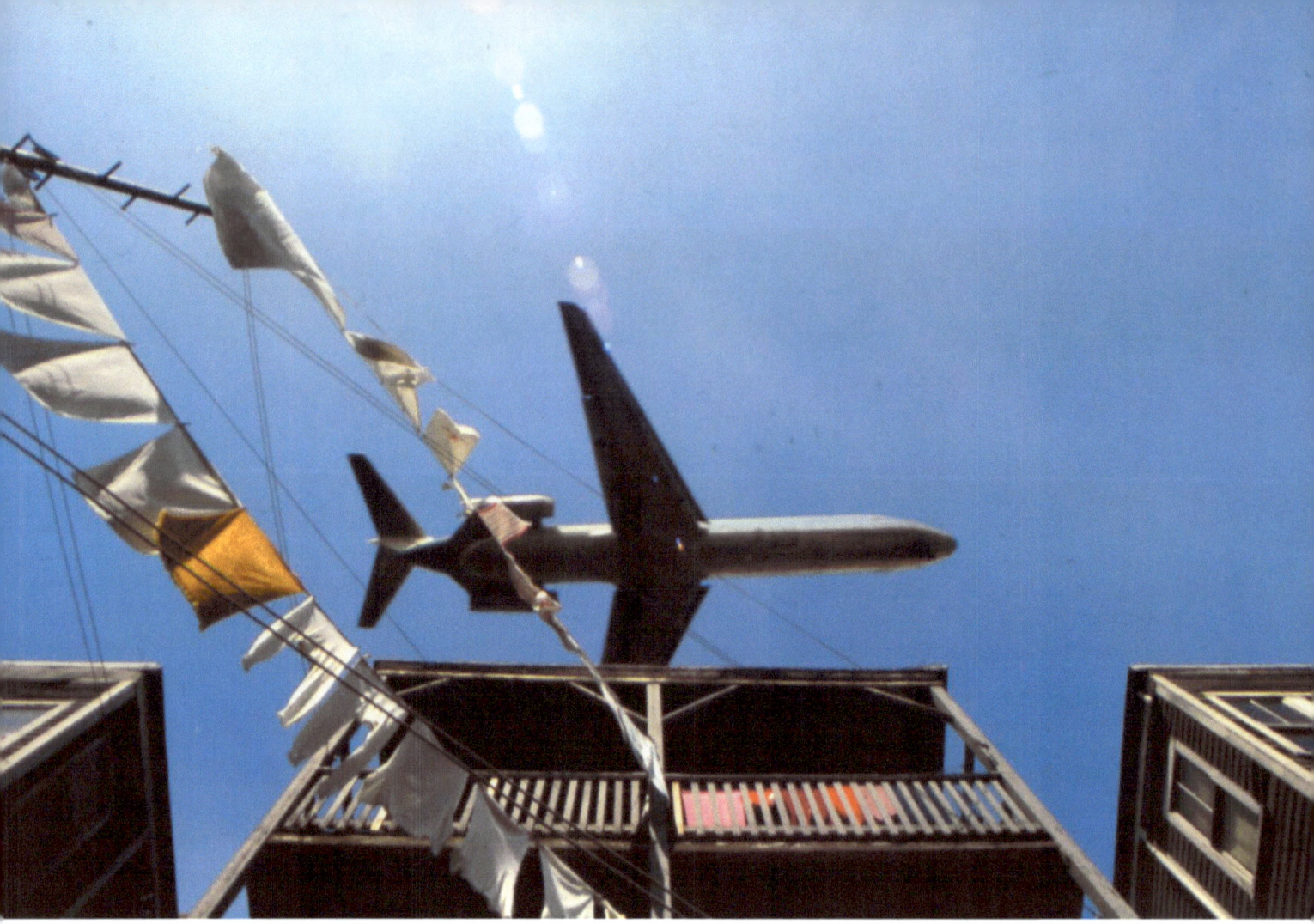

NIMBY (Not In My Back Yard) kept the airplanes over the three-deckers in and around Neptune Road, rather than sharing the noise and fumes with neighboring localities. Later computer programs helped transfer the load by using other flight paths, but much too late for displaced East Boston residents.

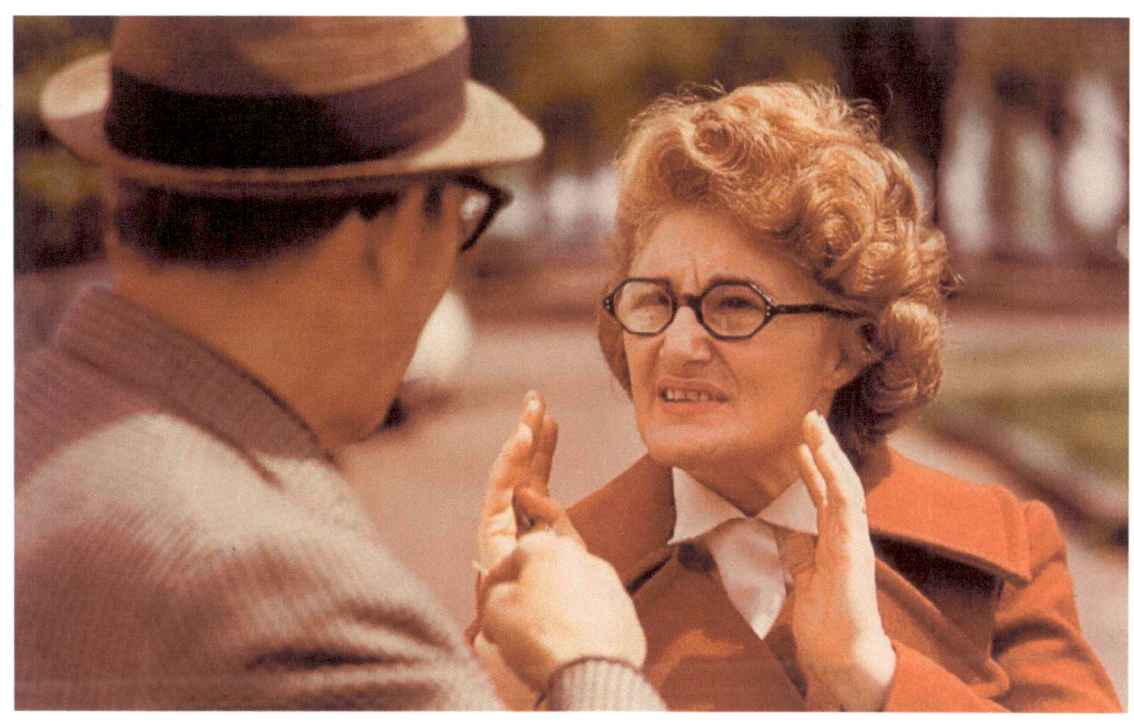

Quality of life becomes diminished when conversations are attempted during what resemble bombing runs. Here, Mary Bruno attempts conversation with Matthew Vieira.

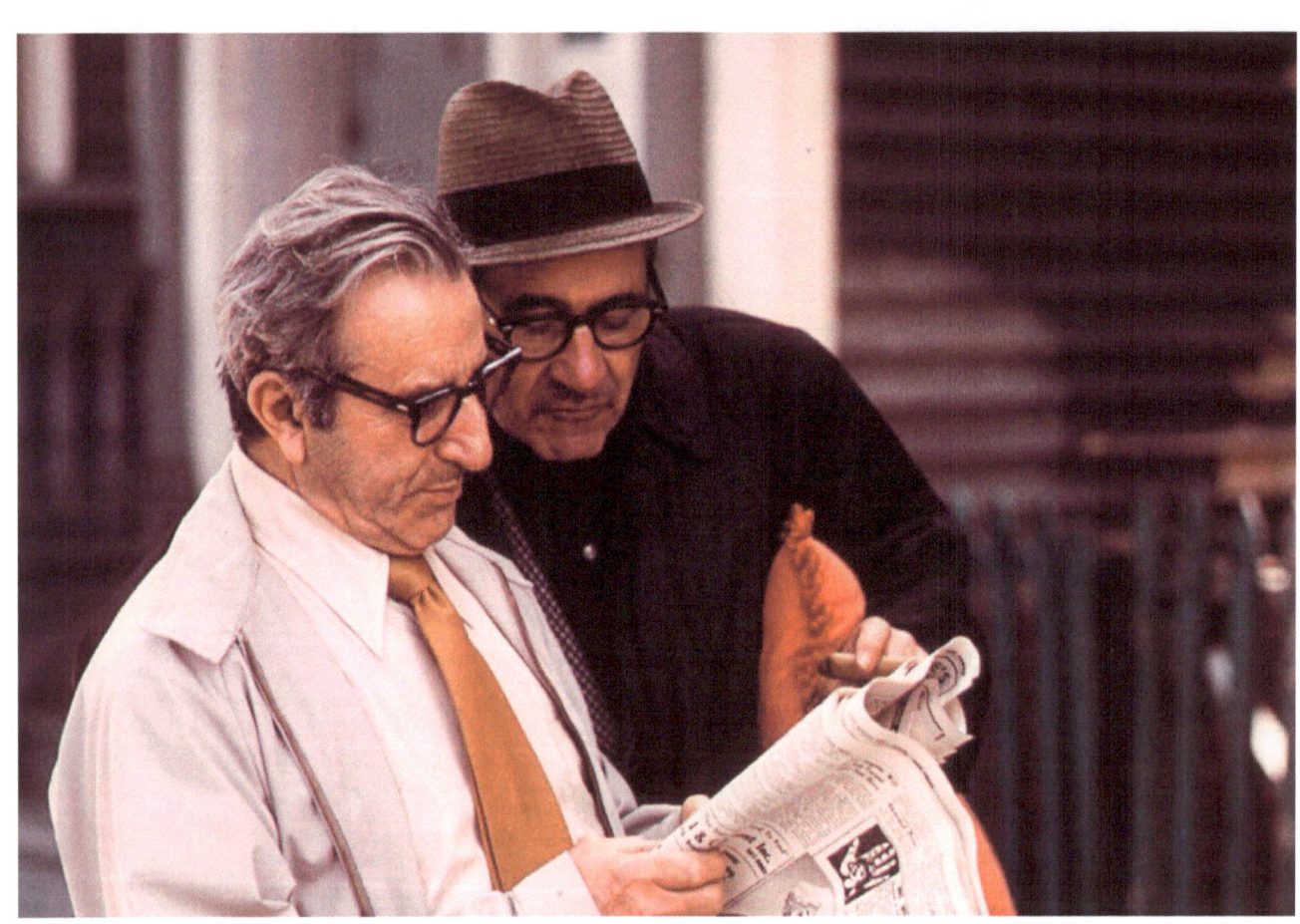

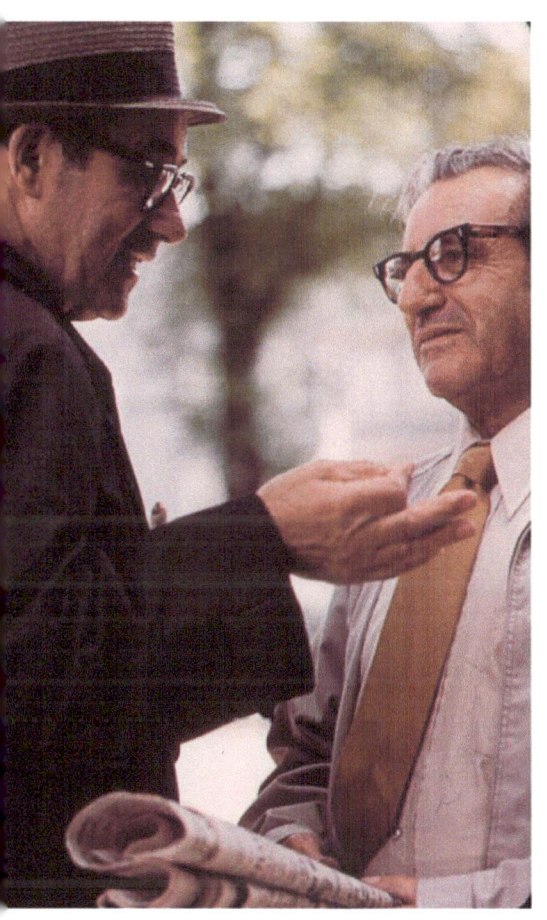

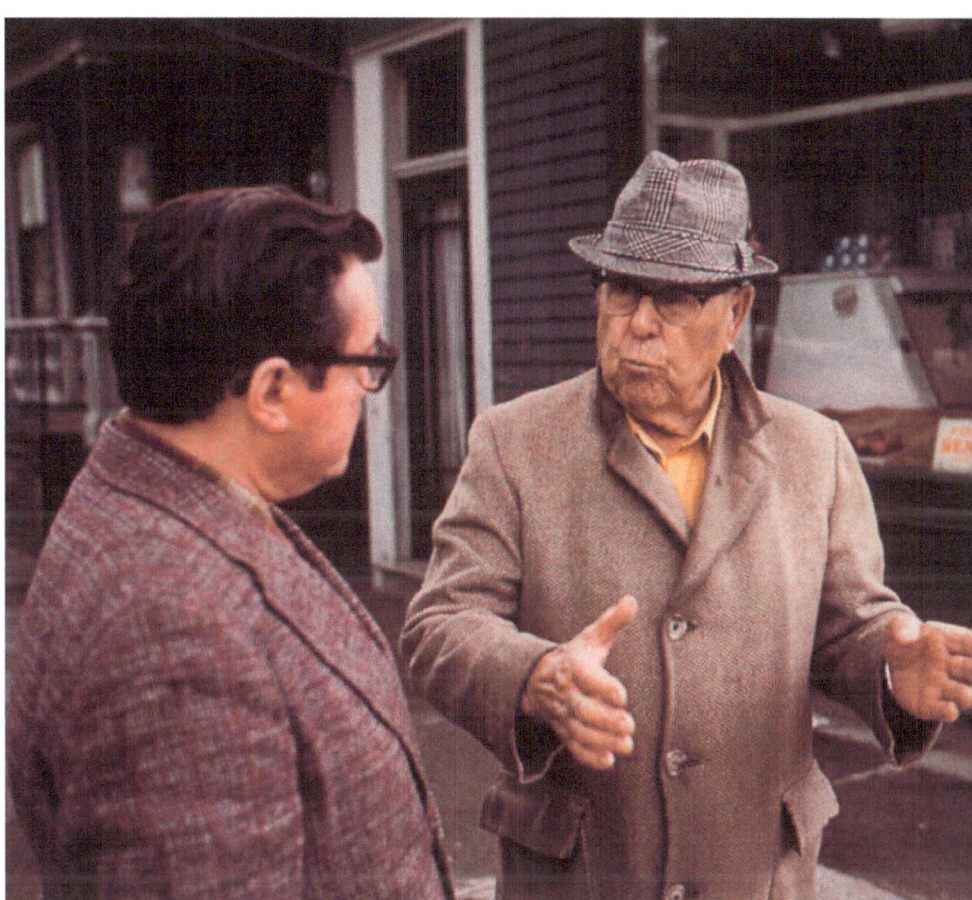

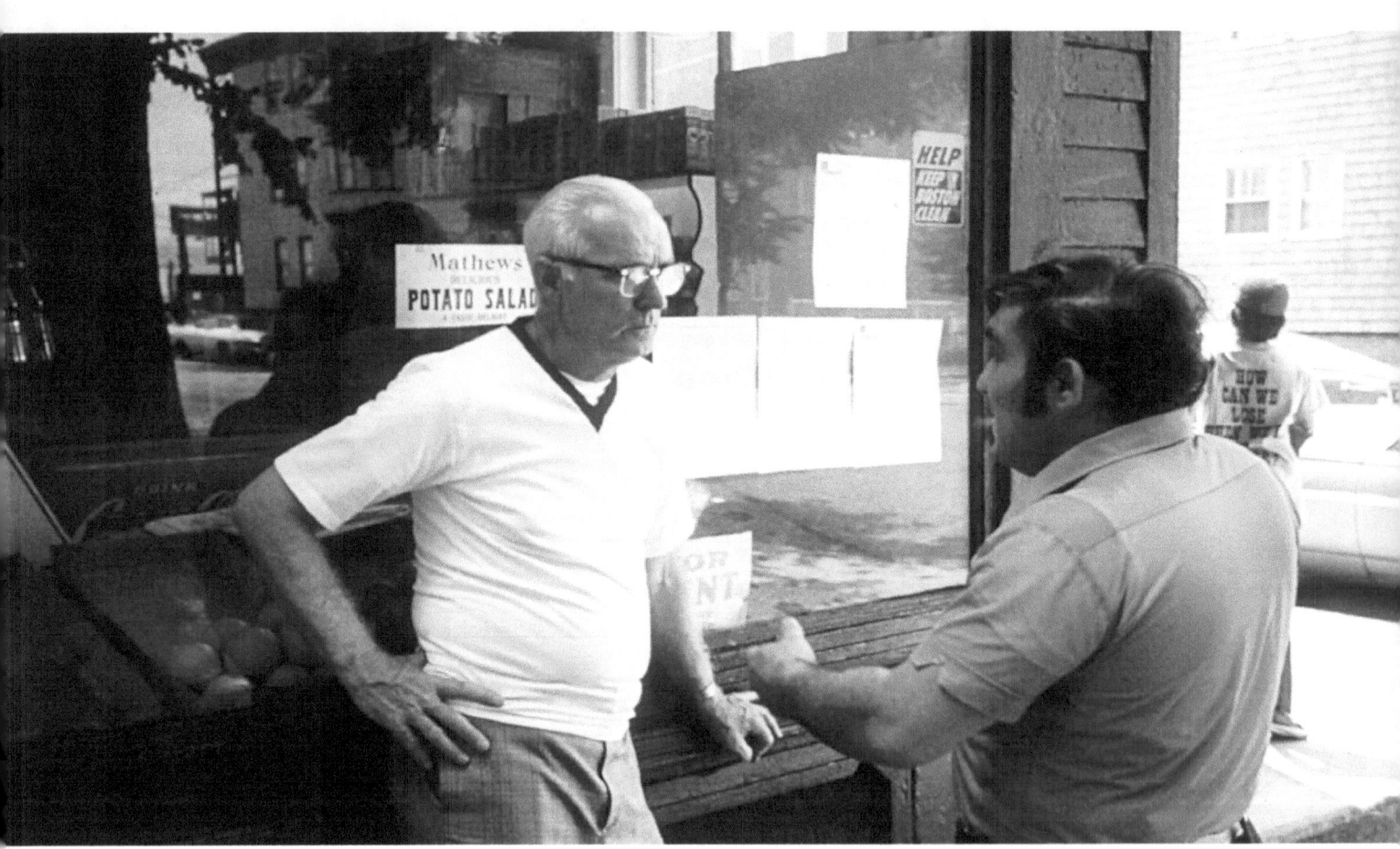

Residents discuss the latest offers to break up the neighborhood.

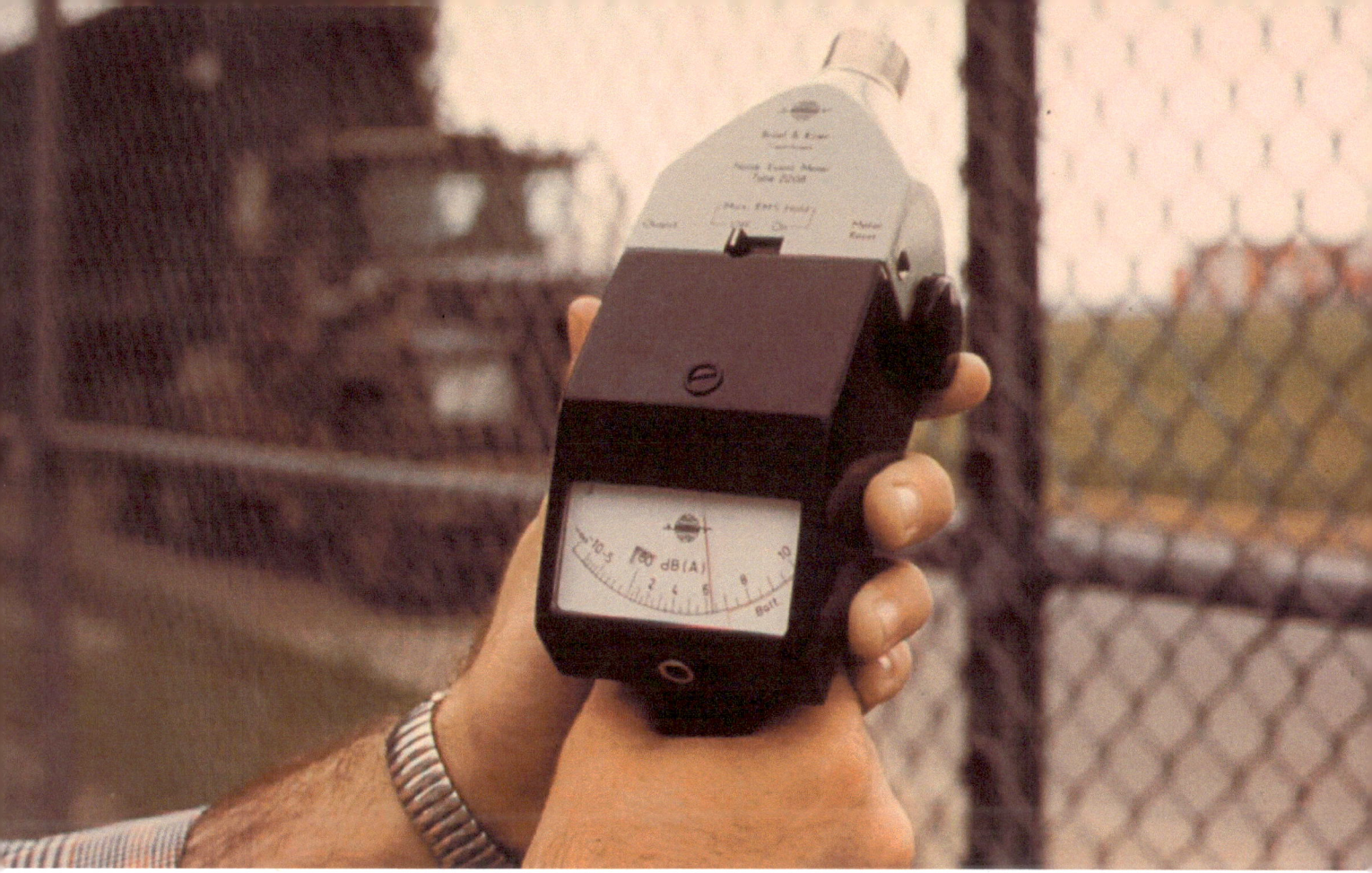

John Vitagliano (in 1973) holds a noise meter used by residents to gauge construction, rapid transit and airplane decibels.

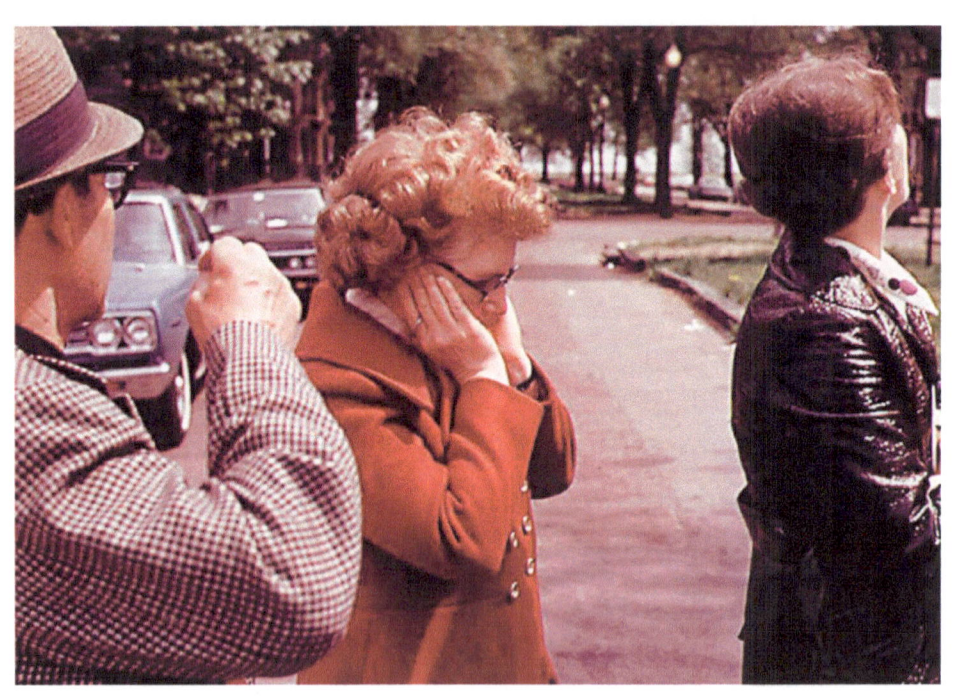

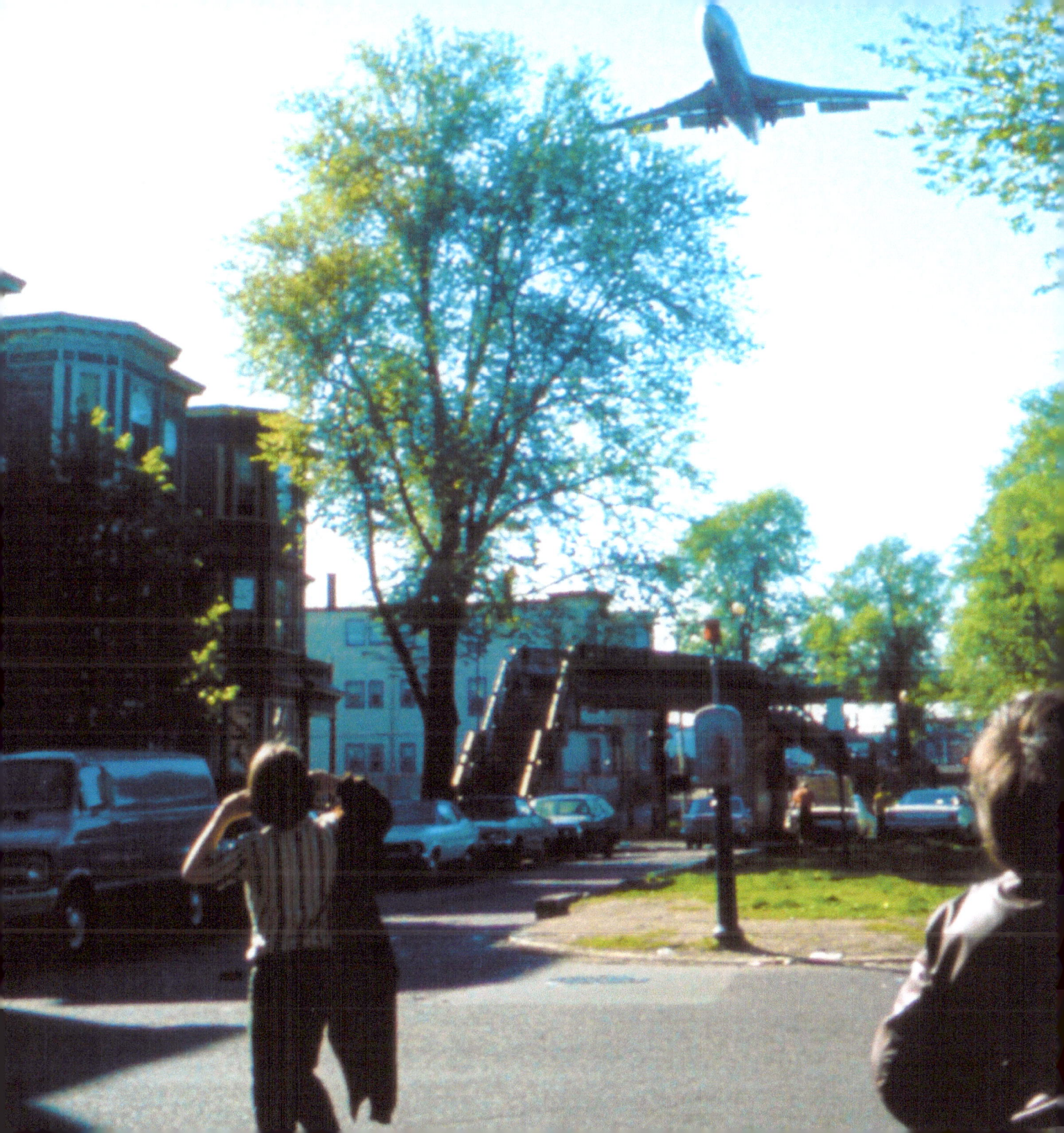

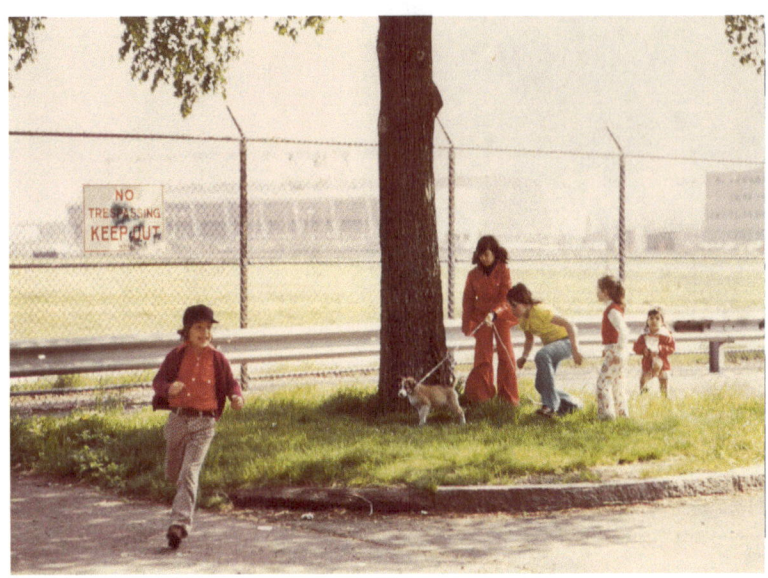

Children play at the airport's expanding border.

On a brisk April morning in 1964, Wood Island Park was destroyed, as King took preemptive action rather than deal responsively with the East Boston community. The destruction came in the person of lumberjacks wielding chain saws, bulldozers churning up grass, and armed police erecting a temporary fence to deny the residents of Neptune Road access to their beloved Wood Island Park.

— John Vitagliano, "Logan Then & Now 1959-1985"

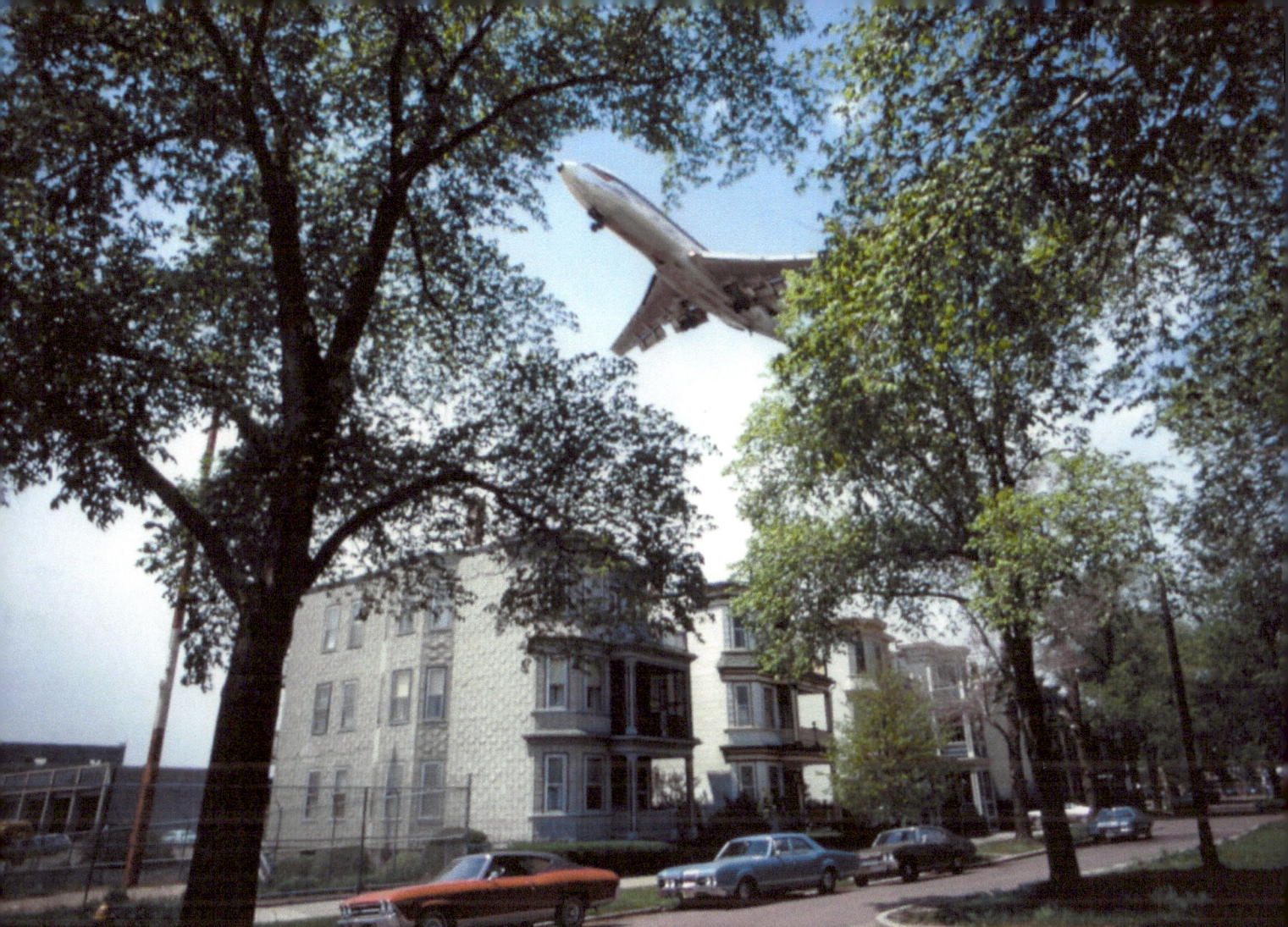

The beautiful neighborhood of three-deckers was systematically reduced by buyouts to empty lots (far left) and systematically confronted with noise pollution, construction pollution, and harassment by public officials intent on removing residents.

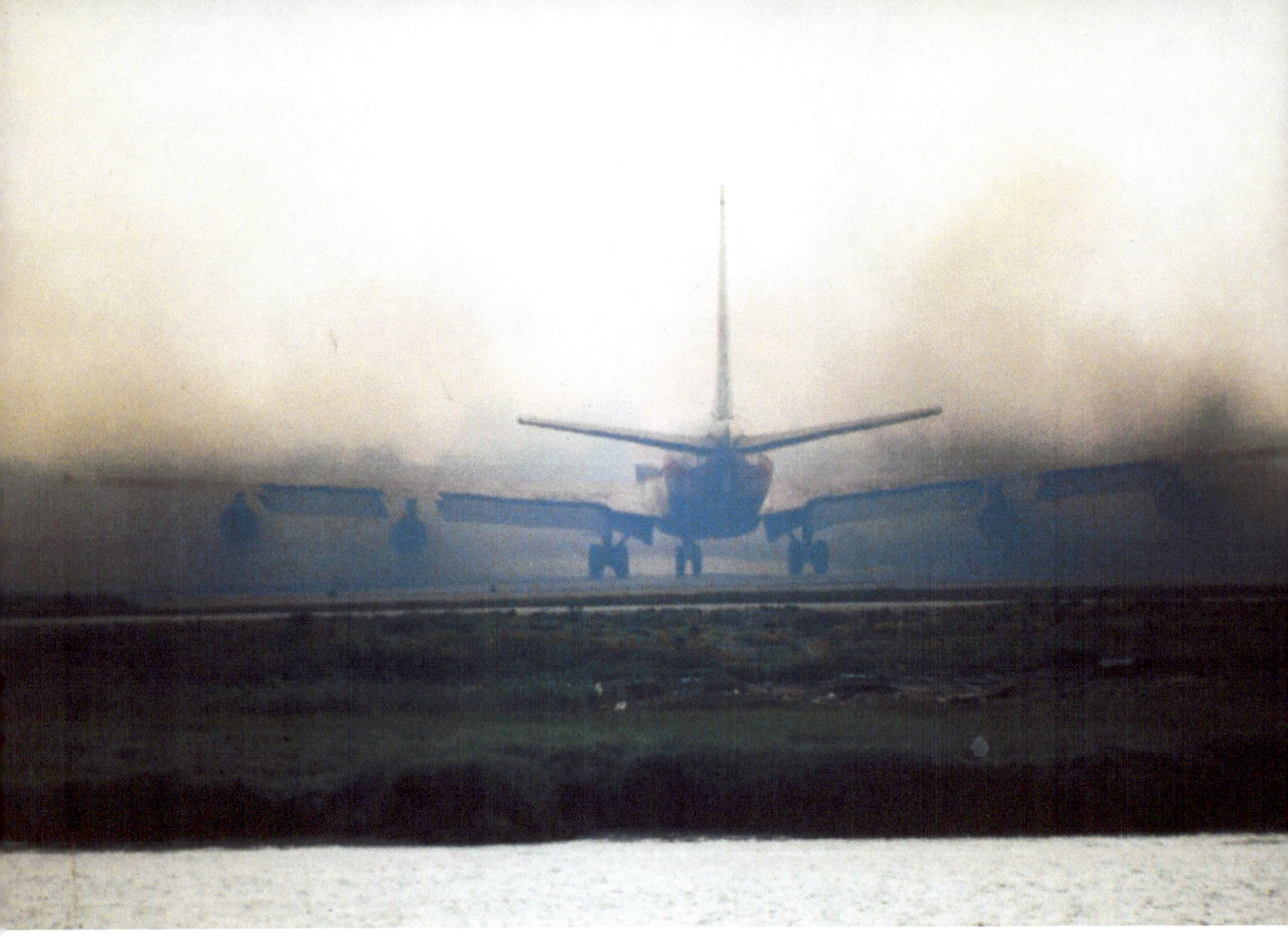

Noise was not the only pollution foisted upon this East Boston community. I recorded stories of eyes tearing from kerosene fumes, broken bones in inner ears, construction vehicle dust and exhaust fumes choking residents, and much more, including heavy trucks (employed by tax-free Massport) wearing down and damaging roads maintained by taxpayers' money.

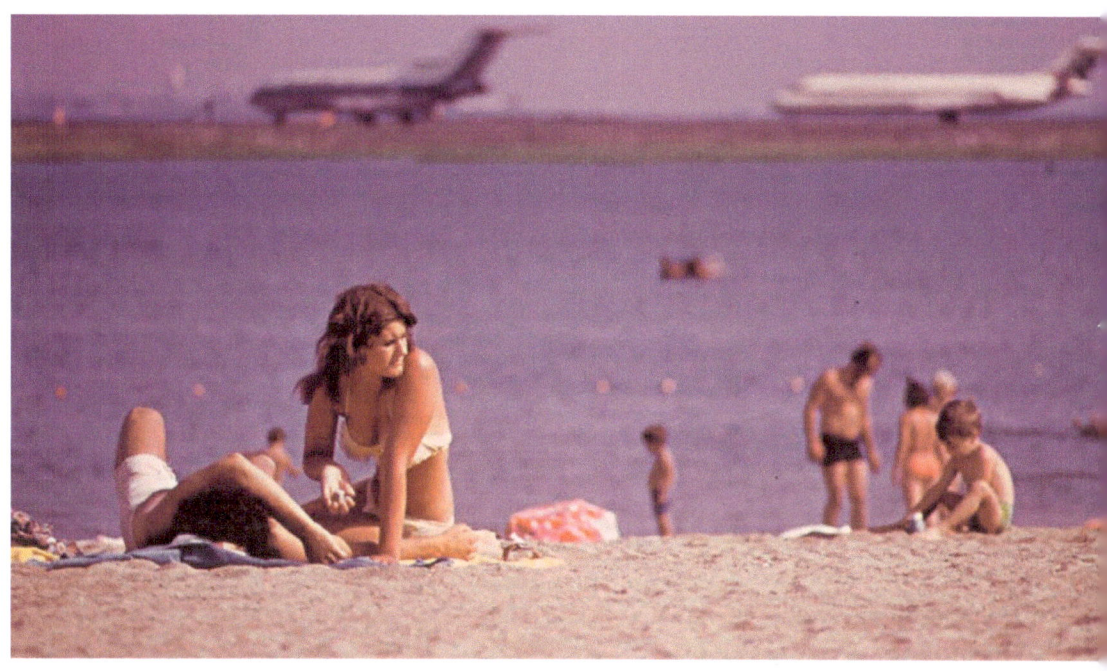

Nearby Constitution Beach was once a destination of serenity for Boston residents.

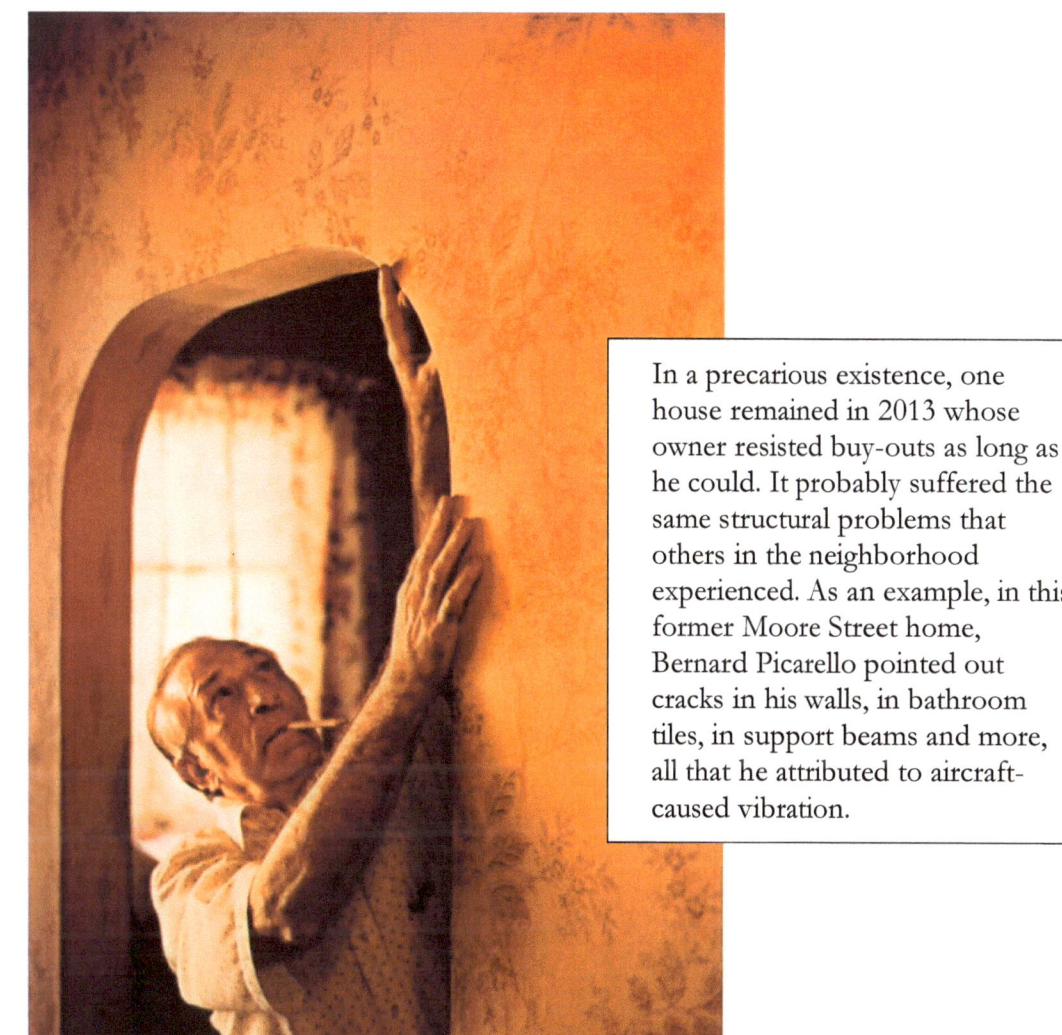

3

last house standing

In a precarious existence, one house remained in 2013 whose owner resisted buy-outs as long as he could. It probably suffered the same structural problems that others in the neighborhood experienced. As an example, in this former Moore Street home, Bernard Picarello pointed out cracks in his walls, in bathroom tiles, in support beams and more, all that he attributed to aircraft-caused vibration.

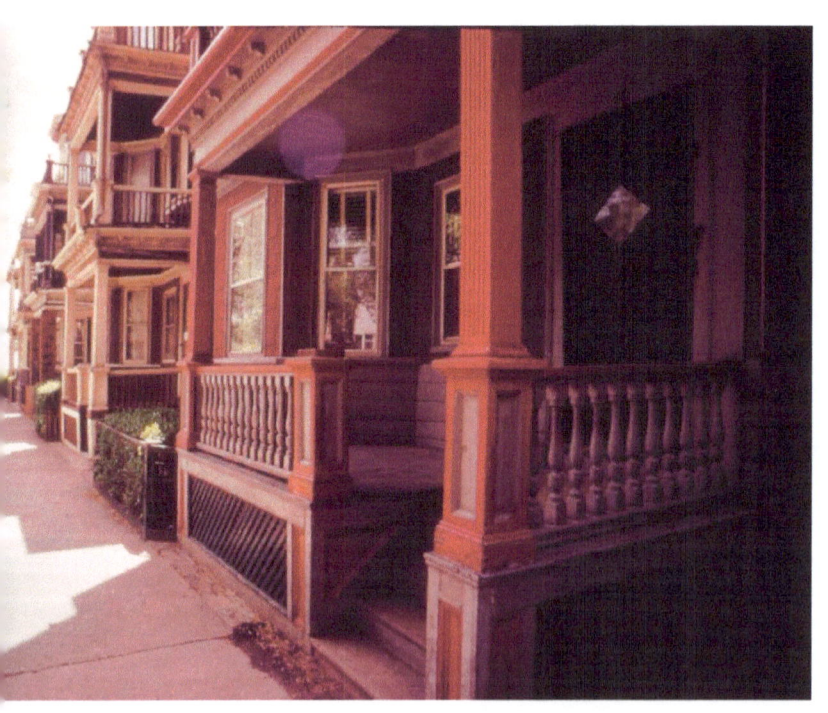

Airport buildings displaced an orchard; a runway covers where Wood Island Park once stood, and airplanes came so close to rooftops that residents petitioned the FAA to allow a 30-foot flag pole with a light on top to be erected on a rooftop close to the runway. This was to indicate to pilots a "height off the roofs." (Landing altitude at that time was not regulated, and depended upon pilot judgment.) Residents, looking for at least that much peace of mind, were told by the FAA that a 12 to 15-foot height would be allowable. A beacon was later erected next to the last house in the row.

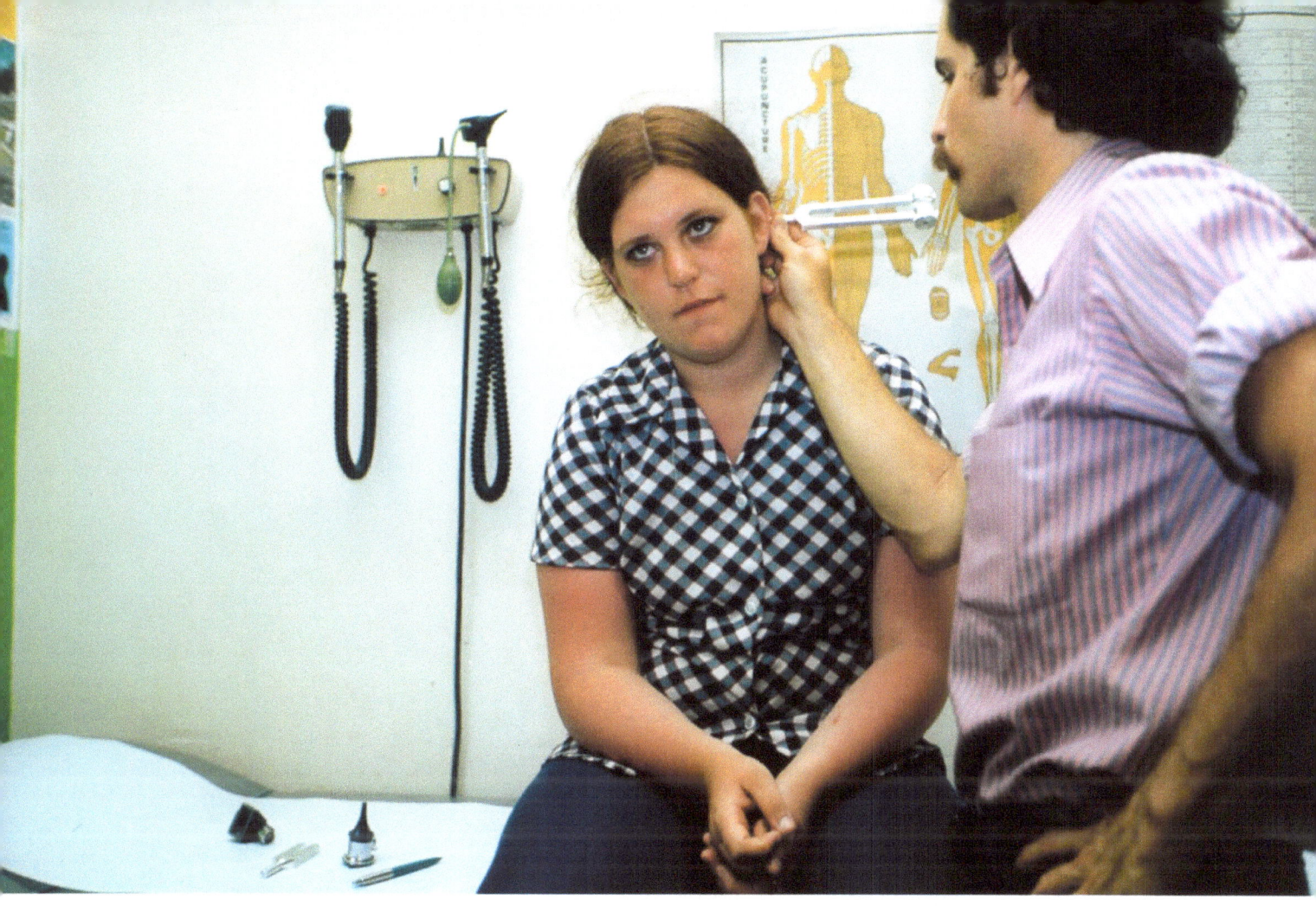

Donna Delaney being examined by Dr. Paul Epstein at a Paris Street Clinic after three prior hearing tests. Referral to a specialist revealed two kinds of hearing loss: one internally caused, the other related to noise.

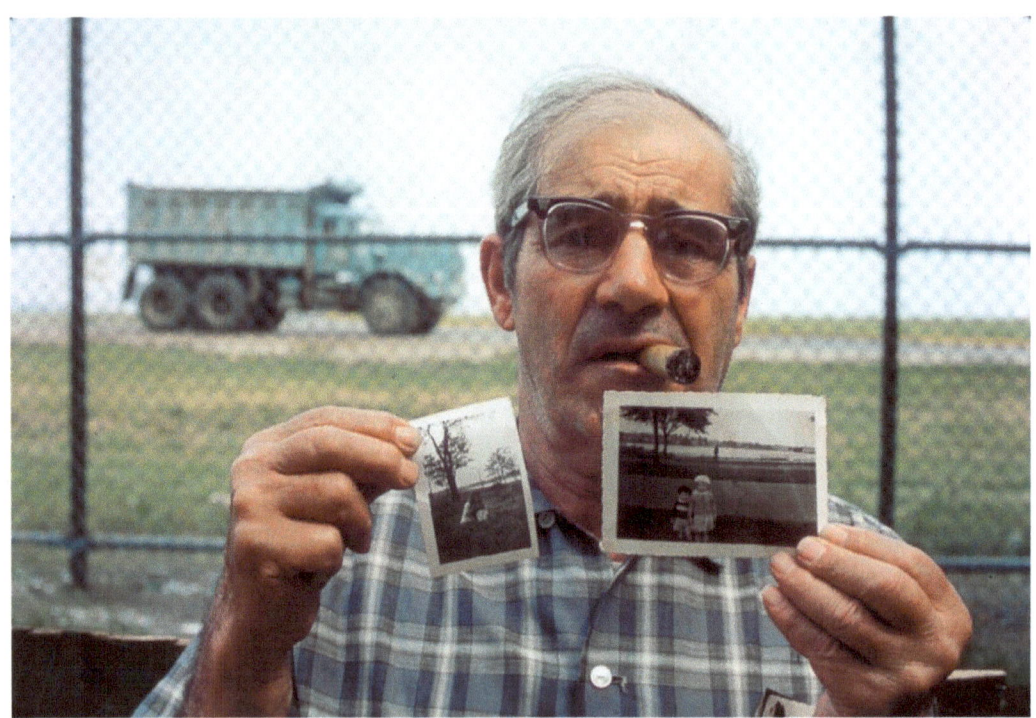

Matthew Vieira holds pictures of his children, taken at Wood Island Park some
35 to 40 years prior. Behind him, the Massport fence across the southeastern end of
Neptune Road and the runway area where Wood Island Park stood. Trucks now
passed back and forth to the newly completed food service building, and to transport
fill, on land taken by the state.

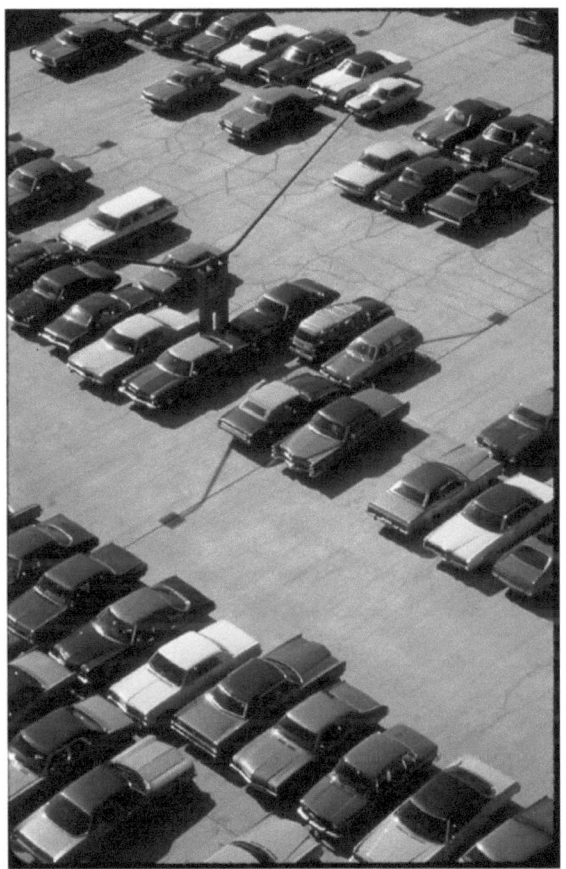

One of the many complaints from residents was
that much land taken away from them was used for
dead storage, including parking, rather than active
aviation use.

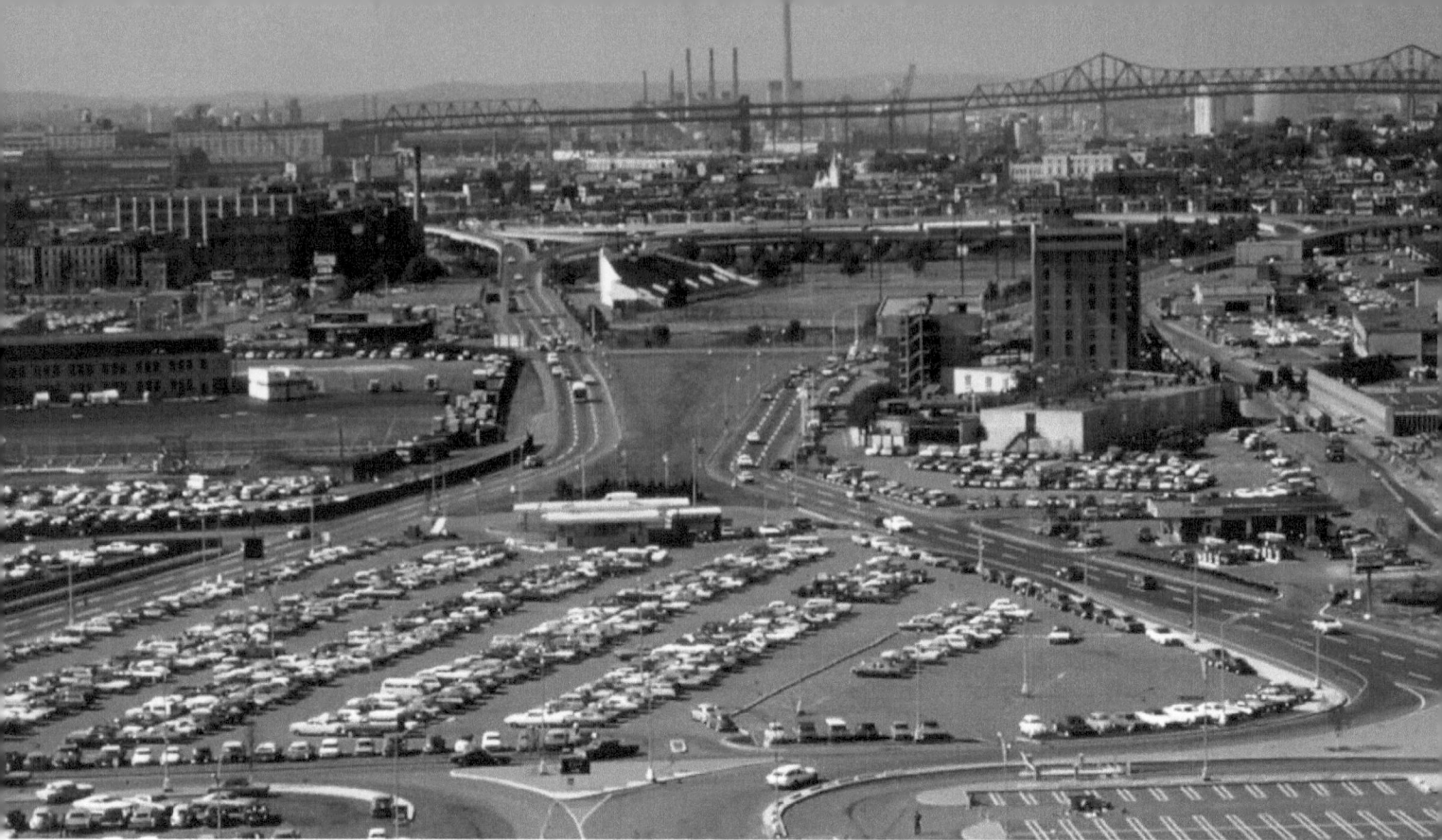

Airport sprawl back then (shown here pushing into the community for parking) was in a location limited for growth: it's at the ocean and has to deal with shipping lanes, and in a densely populated part of the state. It probably should have stayed the regional airport it was meant to be, feeding to another airport with appropriate space inland, perhaps in the Worcester area. By way of comparison, Denver International Airport (DIA) is about 54 square miles, making it the biggest airport in terms of land mass in the U.S. and third largest in the world. DIA is said to be twice the land mass of Manhattan.

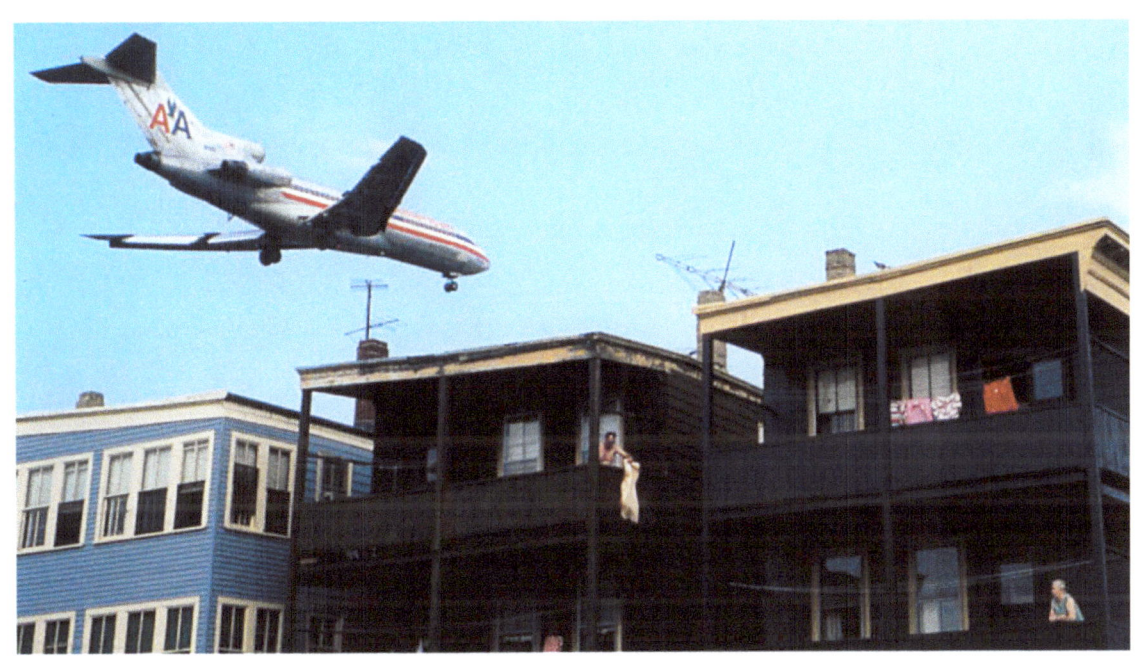

Photographer in Focus – Michael Manheim

by Jeanethe Falvey from the EPA blog "Greenversations" [4]

 Last week, I had the luck of place and time to meet one of the foremost photographers chosen to contribute to Documerica. When photography began in 1972, the Environmental Protection Agency was barely two years into working to better protect public health and the environment. Now, decades later, the inspiration behind this monumental project is once again gaining the attention it deserves.

Each photographer gave us reasons for disbelief and awe, but also for hope. In some places we can see the impact that their raising awareness had. How did you react to these images? In every sense, 'reaction' is a response to some influence or event. Perhaps again, State of the Environment can inspire individual awareness and environmental action the world over.

I met Michael Manheim last week at a gallery talk of his at the Griffin Museum in Belmont, Massachusetts. Among the exhibit of his early work, there quietly hangs one of the more eye-catching moments he caught from East Boston in 1973. Documerica was one of many photography endeavors he took on. Back then he says, "You did whatever it took to keep yourself going." Today, his work reflects the freedom he has to focus deeper (take a look, you'll see). After a lifelong career in photography, any of his images could have been on display. There, when I saw "Landing at Logan," the pride he felt from being a part of Documerica was self-evident.

Like the other photographers, Michael was tasked to submit subject matter of his choice for the project. It was about "connection;" he was excited with "the idea of reaching the public and raising individual awareness." Ultimately, the struggle and anxiety felt by a close-knit community beside Logan Airport drew him in. Relatives from those who lived in the area are still in touch, and his living room photographs leave no doubt that he made the connection he was hoping for. Today most of those houses are gone, replaced by concrete and airport service lots. He wonders what could have been, if he could have raised awareness sooner.

---

4. Greenversations, "Photographer in Focus – Michael Manheim," http://blog.epa.gov/blog/2011/06/michael-manheim (accessed 20 June 2014).

Media Credits

Greenversations: "Photographer in Focus – Michael Manheim"
http://blog.epa.gov/blog/2011/06/michael-manheim

EPA: "Documerica Profile: Michael Philip Manheim"
http://www.youtube.com/watch?v=lxP_scV1s-U

NPR: "Scott Simon Interview with Michael Philip Manheim" (excerpt)
http://www.youtube.com/watch?v=XGvMYuAgneY

Living on Earth: "Documerica" (National Archives curator Bruce Bustard and Michael Manheim)
http://www.loe.org/shows/segments.html?programID=10-P13-00018&segmentID=7

Smithsonian: "Before and After: America's Environmental History"
http://blogs.smithsonianmag.com/artscience/2013/04/before-and-after-americas-environmental-history

U.S. National Archives: "DOCUMERICA - Michael Philip Manheim"
http://www.flickr.com/photos/usnationalarchives/sets/72157620726678645

U.S. National Archives: "DOCUMERICA - Searching for the Seventies"
http://www.youtube.com/watch?v=LHaJmlS7ksI

U.S. National Archives: "DOCUMERICA: The Photographers" (panel discussion)
http://www.ustream.tv/recorded/31641809

Press Release: "National Archives Revisits DOCUMERICA Project with Original Photographers"
http://www.archives.gov/press/press-releases/2013/nr13-85.html

Some online pick-ups
http://cameraclubny.org/ccny_blog/tag/michael-philip-manheim
http://www.rlch.org/news/flickr-photos-help-epa-create-environmental-snapshot
http://www.greenjoyment.com/epa-images-worth-a-thousand-words-answer-the-call
http://www.urbanphoto.net/blog/2010/10/07/life-under-the-landing-gear
http://www.cnsnews.com/news/article/epa-puts-out-global-call-environment-pho

Author Biograpy

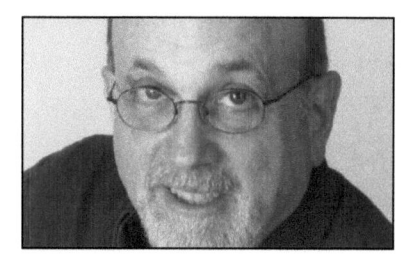

"Photography was a passing interest, at age seven," according to Michael Philip Manheim, "when Cousin Bill gave me a box camera. At age thirteen it kicked in hard."

"I was hooked," he recalled. "I became a kind of local treasure, winning contests with a good eye for composition but a whole lot to learn. I pursued photography with such a passion that it became my profession."

These were exciting years for technical advancements in photographic films and equipment. Creativity was frequently linked to the latest breakthroughs.

Manheim moved past a fascination with equipment for its own sake, learning to pick and choose what he came to regard as tools. He became a professional photographer in 1969.

It took years of experimentation to come up with a personal photographic vision. Manheim began his career as a photojournalist. He went through many phases in his profession, transitioning much later into a focus on themes of change and transformation.

Over the last score of years he developed a signature style of layering multiple exposures of authentic movement onto a single photographic frame. He created an impressionistic approach that transcends the literal.

Michael Philip Manheim's photography has been exhibited throughout the United States and in Germany, Greece, and Italy. His work has been featured in magazines such as *Zoom* (U.S. and Italy), *Photographers International* (Taiwan), *La Fotografia* (Spain), *Black & White* (U.S.), Ballet-Tanz (Germany), and many others.

Manheim's photographs are held in public and private collections. He has been an artist-in-residence at Bates College in Lewiston, Maine and at Phillips Exeter Academy in Exeter, New Hampshire.

www.MichaelPhilipManheim.com

www.behance.net/michaelphilipmanheim

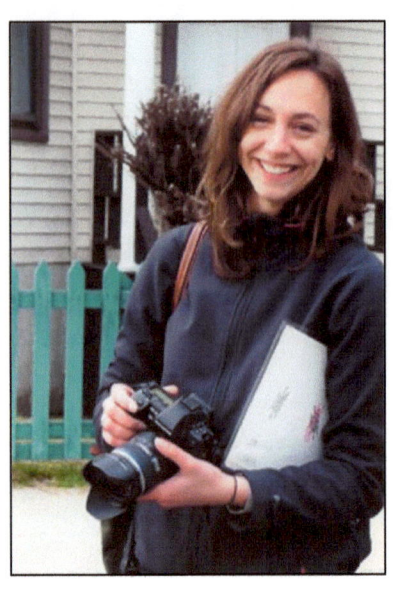

Behind the Scenes,
A Tribute to Jeanethe Falvey

by Michael Philip Manheim

I have encountered a few self-starters in the course of my photojournalism career, people able to serve as a catalyst and put a whole project into being. Jeanethe Falvey is one of those people. There's a DOCUMERICA story, unreported as yet, about this energetic and creative woman who brought this project from the 1970s and 80s into the digital age and raised awareness.

"State of the Environment" was Jeanethe Falvey's idea when she first saw DOCUMERICA's images on the Archives Flickr account. It was her modern call to action, asking the public to emulate what DOCUMERICA's photographers created. One woman's insights and determination brought DOCUMERICA back into view. Jeanethe Falvey at first unknowingly honored Gifford Hampshire's desire to put environmental issues into the public consciousness.

Jeanethe told me that's how she wanted to revive DOCUMERICA, through a public engagement project. She later learned it was exactly what Gifford Hampshire wanted, and she brought it up to date by turning to her version of public crowd sourcing. For Jeanethe, it just made sense to reach out to the public at large. She created a two-part program to reach out all over the world. She wisely set up an online showcase for amateur photographers, making it easy and desirable for them to get involved. Here is the story in her own words:

"A lucky conversation I had with individuals at the National Archives unlocked a forgotten time capsule of our country. Suddenly, over 22,000 images—and with them the emotions, the stories, the intent—came flooding back to life. Anyone, anyone passionate about our world would feel the impact of the photos as I did.

"The black smoke, the poisoned rivers, the faces of the people struck me. They were living in a time when our country had finally taken a stand, because the state of the environment was not acceptable for its people. A new and healthier quality of life was around the corner.

"I knew immediately that we had to do it again. Not only did I want to revisit the tremendous foresight of Gifford Hampshire and his photographers, but I wanted the world to see how far we had come, and more clearly see what we might face ahead.

"My idea was simple: showcase the historic photos, showcase the stories and communities documented all those years ago, and revisit those places today and document the change—through social media—with the help of the public.

I have been hopeful that State of the Environment's images from across our world will make a second and lasting statement about our choices of the past that have created our current quality of life. I hope that, like DOCUMERICA, we now capture our current global challenges and our current responses to those challenges, which will ultimately shape the quality of life for our future."

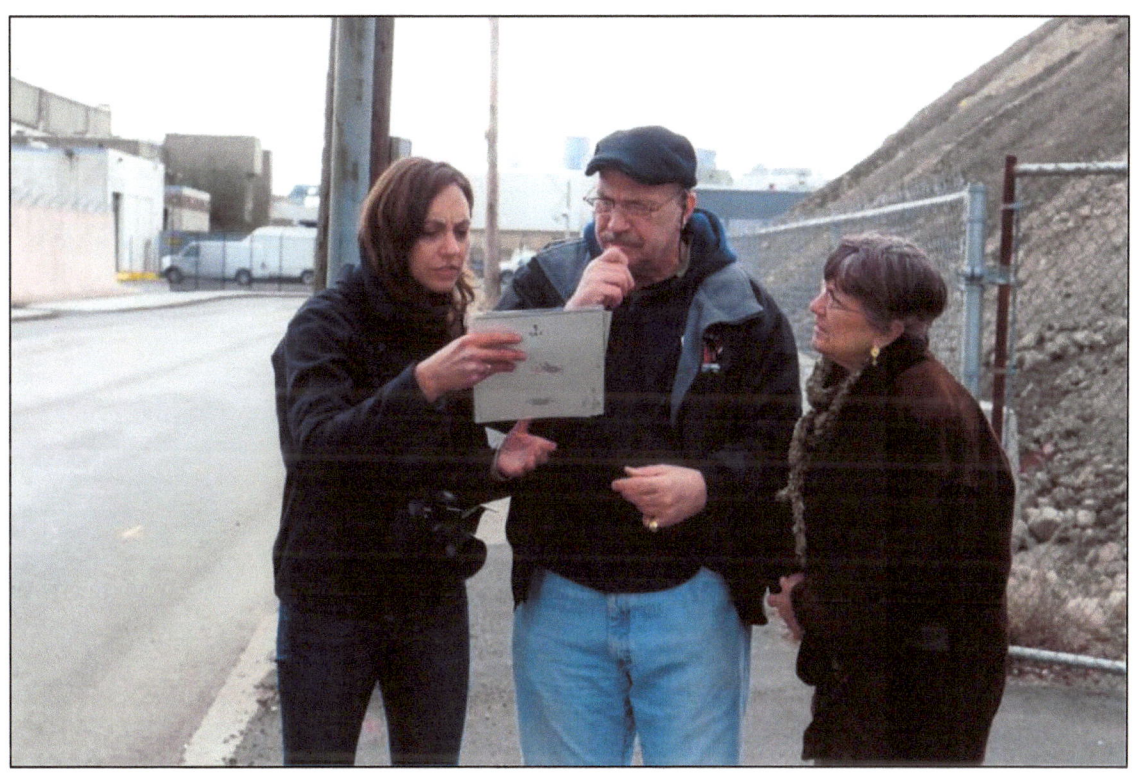

Jeanethe Falvey consults with some of the former area residents, reviewing how once they lived in an enclave of three-decker homes on a tree-lined street just a walk away from Olmsted's Wood Island Park.

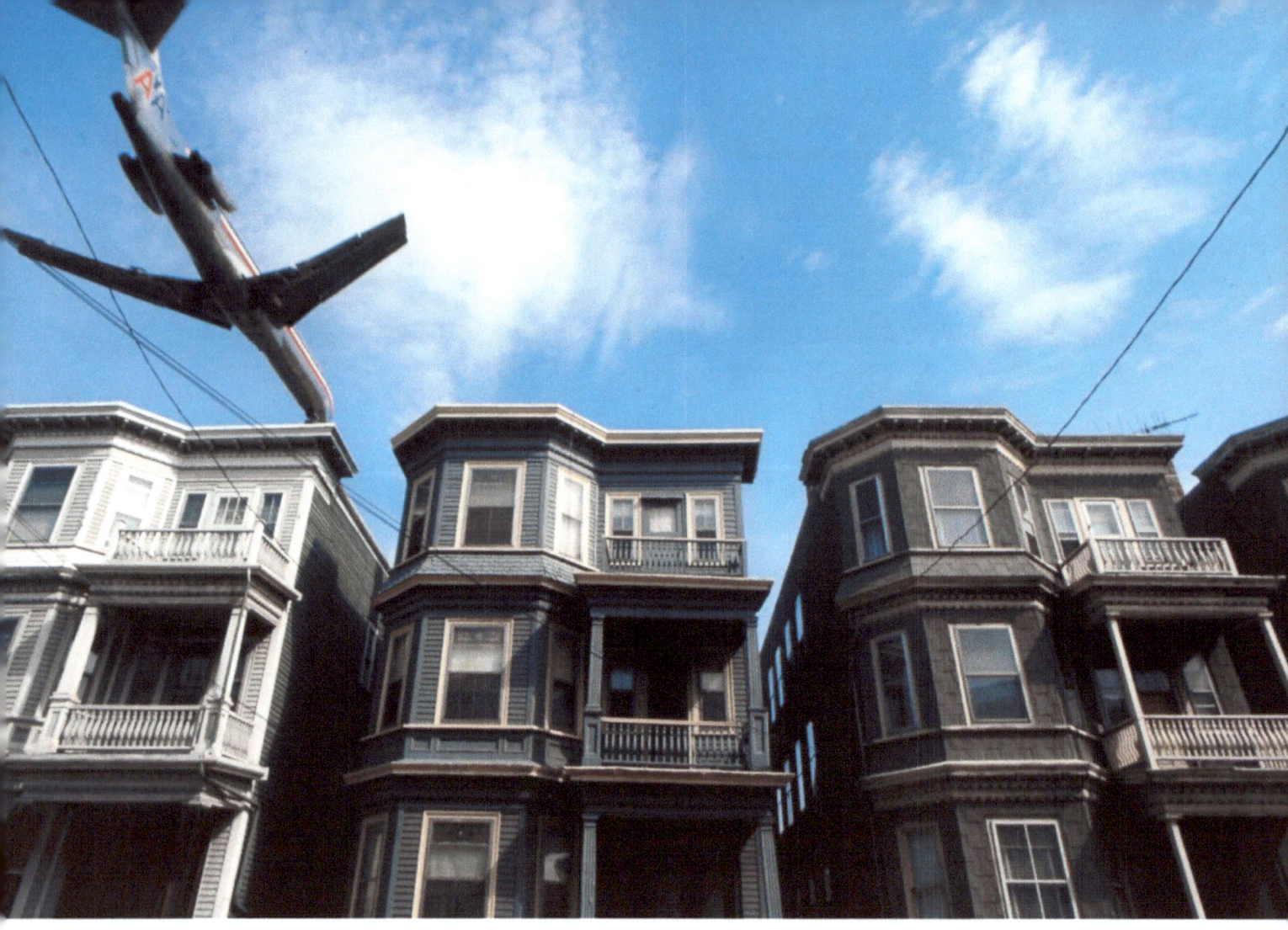

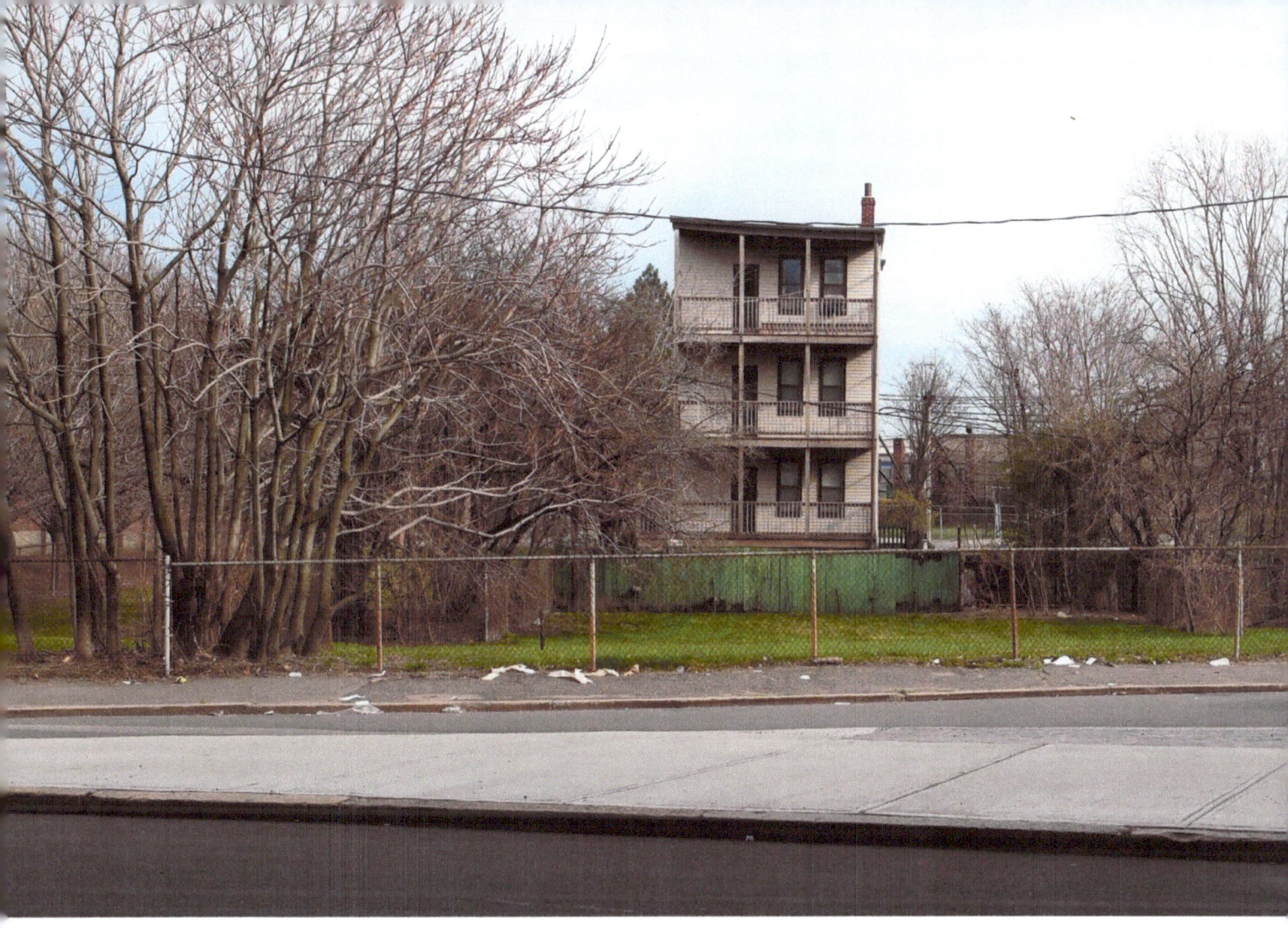

www.ingramcontent.com/pod-product-compliance
Lightning Source LLC
Chambersburg PA
CBHW050900180526
45159CB00007B/2737